Meeting the Nutritional Needs

of

<u>YOUR</u> Breed of Dog

Doral Publishing, Inc.

Published by Doral Publishing, Inc., 8560 SW Salish Lane #300, Wilsonville, Oregon 97070-9612

Copyedited by Alvin Grossman
Book Design by Graphica Pacific Design

Library of Congress Card Number: 97-65218
ISBN: 0-944875-50-5

Cusick, William D.
        Meeting the Nutritional Needs of Your Breed of Dog /
William D. Cusick. — Wilsonville, OR :
Doral Pub., 1997

p. : ill.   cm.

Includes Index
ISBN: 0-944875-50-5

1. Dogs—Feeding and feeds.   2. Dogs—Food
—Recipes.   I. Title

SF427.4.C   636.7'085

                                            00-

Foreword

This book is a comprehensive study of specialized nutritional needs that vary from breed to breed.

This book will show dog owners why dogs taken out of their natural habitat and fed a diet containing food sources unsuitable for their specific systems will develop nutritional allergies. It gives the dog owner a simple solution to this common problem, which can be manifested by body rashes, pigmentation changes, or coat loss. This information also explains why the nutrient source for a commercial all-breed dog food satisfactory for one breed may cause nutritional problems for a different breed of dog.

With Special Thanks

TO SANDY

Without you this book would not have been finished

Also
To the many dog breeders who spent their time sharing
their knowledge and in some cases risking the health of their dogs

Warning - Disclaimer

This book is designed to provide information in regard to the subject matter covered. It is sold with the understanding that the publisher and author are not engaged in rendering veterinary, medical or other professional services. If veterinary or other expert assistance is required, the services of a competent professional should be sought.

It is not the purpose of this manual to reprint all the information that is otherwise available to the author and/or publisher, but to complement, amplify and supplement other text. You are urged to read all the available material, learn as much as possible about canine nutrition and to tailor the information to your individual needs.

Every effort has been made to make this manual as complete and as accurate as possible. However, **there may be mistakes** both typographical and in content. Therefore, this text should be used only as a general guide and not as the ultimate source of information on canine nutrition. Furthermore, this manual contains information on canine nutrition only up to the printing date.

The purpose of this manual is to educate and entertain. The author and publisher shall have neither liability nor responsibility to any person or entity with respect to any loss or damage caused, or alleged to be caused, directly or indirectly by the information contained in this book.

If you do not wish to be bound by the above, you may return this book to the publisher for a full refund.

BASIC NUTRITION

CONTENTS

Breed by Breed
(Continued)

HOW DIFFERENT BREEDS DEVELOPED DIFFERENT NUTRITIONAL NEEDS

It is truly fascinating to see a 235-pound Irish Wolfhound standing beside a 5-pound Pekingese, an Alaskan Malamute, and a Dachshund. When different breeds are standing side by side, it is sometimes hard to comprehend that they all belong to one single species of animal. There are over 250 different breeds within that one single species called canine. Each breed is unique; each differs in its appearance, its temperament, and its nutritional needs. How did these many breeds become so differentiated?

To understand the development of the variations found in modern day dogs, we must go back before the time man first became involved with these animals, just a short 10,000 years ago. The actual evolution of modern day dogs began over 40 million years ago! It is by going back and researching dogs' evolution over these last 40 million years that we gain insight into how the modern breeds of today became so differentiated.

None of us questions the difference in coats between an arctic breed and a breed from the desert. Most of us also accept the theory of how different breeds developed different coats to survive within a specific environment. In the arctic the extremely low temperatures created a requirement for a thick double coat to protect the dog in its cold climate. In the desert the hot arid temperatures created a requirement for a lighter single coat. Thus, the dog's survival in these different climates dictated the development of a suitable coat.

We also should not be surprised to find different nutritional requirements among breeds from different environments. Like the way an environment's climate effected the development of a dog's coat, that same environment effected the development of a dog's nutritional requirements. The native nutrients found in Nordic tundra and ice are different from the nutrients found in the sand of the desert. Therefore, as each type of dog developed within a specific environment, its survival also depended upon the dog's ability to process that environment's food. Thus exposure to different environments produced breeds of dogs with as many variations in nutritional requirements as they have variations in appearance.

When comparing two breeds, often the differences can be more easily identified if each breed has remained within a specific type of environment for a prolonged time. For example, comparing exterior differences between any one of the Nordic breeds and the Pharaoh Hound is obvious. The Nordic breeds all developed in cold climates. The Pharaoh Hound developed in the arid regions south of the Mediterranean and was even isolated on a single Mediterranean island for thousands of years. Since we know of this isolation we also can identify the Pharaoh Hound's specific developmental native nutrients. Knowing both the Pharaoh Hound's present nutritional requirements and their native island's specific nutrients, we can see the association between these two known facts. We also can show how this isolation, by limiting the breed to specific nutrients, produced very pronounced breed specific nutritional requirements.

With breeds that are new genetic hybrids, it is also possible to identify the environments and the native nutrients that played a role in the creation of their nutritional requirements. However, to accomplish this we must be able to trace their family tree. An example of this would be our tracing the development of the Sealyham Terrier, which was created by Captain John Edwards in the late 1800's. Since Captain Edwards kept very accurate records of his breeding efforts in the development of the Sealyham Terrier, the process of tracing its family tree is easy. With other genetic hybrids this process can be much more difficult, and with some breeds all that can be done is offer an educated guess.

When considering the history of nutritional development for the members of the dog family, another lesson we can learn from close inspection of each breed is; be careful not to assume that all dogs from a specific country, *as we know it today*, have the same nutritional heritage. A dog from China could be from the Mandarin, Hunan, or Szechuan province. A dog from a smaller country, such as Germany, could have come from a mountain environment, middle elevation plateaus, or a lowland area next to the Baltic Sea. A dog from Italy could have come from the Sicilian or the Castilian Province. Within each country there may be different environments. These in turn have their own unique foods. Thus, breeds developing in the different environments of a single country would have developed different nutritional requirements.

Also, to believe that all desert breeds or all mountain breeds have the same nutritional needs is wrong. We would have to be more specific. Are the nutrients found in a high desert or a low desert environment?

Or if you are referring to the Alps of Germany, Switzerland or France as *The Mountains*, consider this: *The tallest mountain in the French Alps is Mont Blanc reaching 15,771 feet above sea level. The top of this mountain is lower than the average elevations (16,000 feet above sea level) for the Plateau Area of Tibet. The mountains of Tibet go up from this country's "lower" plateau's to an elevation of over 29,000 feet high. The nutrients found on the mountains of Tibet are very different from the nutrients found on Mont Blanc.* Therefore, when considering the environment where a specific breed of dog developed, we must look beyond the geographic label of *mountain, plateau* or *desert* to identify the nutrients from that specific breed's area of origin.

Now let us consider the length of time that it would take to make a genetic change, due to an environmental change for any of today's breeds of dog. Man has written about specific breeds of dog for the last 8000 years, but not one word can be found showing that a single breed of dog has changed its genetic make-up due to a change in its environment in all this time. On the other hand many written accounts of breeds show they remain the same, even after prolonged exposure to a new and different environment. One example of non-change after prolonged exposure to a new environment is in the written records of the Whippet. These records indicate the Whippet, which was transported from a hot and dry homeland to England's cold and damp climate in 49 A.D., was very much the same then as today's Whippet. This breed has retained a short sleek coat developed for a hot and dry climate, even after 2,100 years of being bred true in a cold and damp climate. Thus, the Whippet by retaining its short sleek coat, is evidence to us that the length of time it can take to make an evolutionary change due to environmental effect can be over 2,100 years.

The length of time needed to make a nutritional requirement change due to exposure to a new environment's food supply also can take thousands of years. This is why today's Alaskan Malamute (a Nordic breed) still thrives on fish, the German Shepherd Dog (a low plains farmland breed) still thrives on beef and grain, and the Greyhound (a desert breed) still thrives on rabbit. These breeds, like all the different breeds removed from their native environment and exposed to a single food supply (ie. one processed dog food formula), cannot have their nutritional needs satisfactorily fulfilled. **Each breed has retained the genetic differences that it developed in its distinctly different native environments** and for this reason, each should be treated NUTRITIONALLY as the individual that it is.

3

Each breed of dog has

physical or temperamental characteristics

that are different from any other breed.

The question is

NOT IF *those characteristics affect*

a breed's nutritional requirements,

BUT HOW MUCH *do they affect a*

breed's nutritional requirements?

WE SHOULD KNOW:

A breed that sheds

would need different amounts

of coat producing nutrients

than a breed that does not shed.

BREED SPECIFIC U. S. GOVERNMENT RESEARCH

In the early 1970's the government's National Research Council formed a subcommittee to study the nutritional requirements of dogs. The President at that time was L. B. Johnson. It was at his specific request that this subcommittee was formed and research documentation compiled. Also noteworthy is the fact that the President and his wife Ladybird Johnson owned and raised Beagles. That is why most of the research for the first report by this newly formed subcommittee was related to nutritional requirements of the Beagle. The subcommittee published their report "Minimum Nutrient Requirements of Dogs for Growth and Maintenance" in 1974. Later in 1980 and again in 1985 their expanded revisions showed tests on more nutrients and used different breeds. In the 1985 revision many multi breed research studies cited led the committee to state *"requirement of the dog can also vary depending on the methods and criteria used in their derivation."* Or in lay terms, different breeds of dogs can have different nutritional requirements due to where and how a specific breed developed.

In the National Research Council's 1985 report there are many hundreds of research studies cited from schools of veterinary medicine, dog food companies, and independent laboratories. Each of these studies pertains to a single nutrient, ie; vitamin A, calcium, copper, etc. With each research study, when two or more breeds were used, it also showed their nutritional differences. Very noteworthy is the fact that **in the entire 1985 report not one research study cited showed two breeds to have the same nutritional requirements for any one nutrient**.

Samples of specific research confirming breed specific nutritional differences are found throughout the NRC's 1985 revised Nutrient Requirements of Dogs:

Specific test that show different breeds of dogs all have different nutritional needs can be seen in tests cited on the following pages: Page 3: "These data illustrate the marked effect on energy requirements imposed by the environment and the additional influence of differences in breed and behavior." Page 9: "Estimates of the protein requirement of the dog can also vary depending on the methods and criteria used in their derivation." Page 11: "Blaza et al. (1982) studied the sulfur amino acid requirements of growing Labrador and Beagle dogs in three experiments... These studies indicated that the dog's breed may influence methionine requirements, since Labradors but not Beagles responded to increasing the methionine content from 0.36 to 0.71 percent by increased weight gains and food intakes." Page 16: In the section on Calcium... "Dogs of some types and breeds may perform satisfactorily on lower intakes of these minerals."... "It is recognized that there are many breeds of dogs, that they are maintained under a wide range of environments, and are being... " Page 19: "Tinedt et al. (1979) reported a copper toxicosis in Bedlington Terriers fed commercial dog diets containing 5 to 10 mg. copper per kilogram of diet. Ludwig et al. (1980) studied this disease in considerable detail and concluded that it is unique to this breed of dog and is caused by a genetic abnormality." ... "The copper requirements for the majority of dog breeds appears to be quite low." Page 20: "Sanecki et al. (1982) fed English Pointer pups a corn-soy based zinc-deficient diet and reported observing within 5 weeks lesions of ... These lesions were reversible by adding 200 mg. zinc carbonate per kilogram to the diet, with complete remission of the external lesions in 6 weeks".... "Fisher (1977) fed more than 800 Beagles 32 mg./kg zinc of diet (calcium concentration not noted) and did not report any clinical signs of zinc deficiency." Page 24: "Kozelka et al. (1933) found that Collie puppies were protected from rickets by a 1 to 1.3 IU vitamin D (irradiated ergosterol) per kilogram of body weight per day. Arnold and Elvehjem (1939) found calcification to be normal in a growing Airedale puppy receiving a 1.39 percent calcium and a 1.05 percent phosphorus (Ca/P = 1.32:1) diet and 132 IU or less of vitamin D per kilogram of body weight per day showed that growth and bone mineralization were normal." ... "Fleischmann Laboratories (1944) reported that 28 IU vitamin D per kilogram of body weight daily was sufficient for Fox Terriers when using a dietary calcium:phosphorus ratio of 2.1:1. However, even with 270 IU per kilogram of body weight per day, Collies and Great Danes showed X-ray evidence of rickets."

Every few years the Board Members of the National Research Council compiled the research data. They then reviewed all the specific tests. After this review, they recommended the minimum amounts of each nutrient for commercial dog food within the United States. The recommended nutrient amounts are the quantities determined by the committee to sustain life at a safe level and balance for any or all breeds of dog. These recommended amounts are called the "Minimum Nutrient Requirements of Dogs for Growth and Maintenance (amounts per Kilogram of body weight per day)" or "Required Minimum Concentrations of Available Nutrients in Dog Food Formulated for Growth."

Each breed of dog has

physical or temperamental characteristics

that are different from any other breed.

The question is

NOT IF *those characteristics affect*

a breed's nutritional requirements,

BUT HOW MUCH *do they affect a*

breed's nutritional requirements?

WE SHOULD KNOW:

A dog with a coat weighing 10% of its overall weight

will need more of the nutrients

that grow and maintain coat hair

than a dog with a coat weighing 5% of its overall weight.

NUTRITIONAL TEAMWORK

When inspecting each essential nutrient in a dog's diet, it is very important to look at the other nutrients they affect or that affect them. The nutrients that work together are the NUTRITIONAL TEAMS. We all recognize the teamwork between water and solid foods in the dog's diet. If either one is not present, we know the result will be death due to a lack of an essential part of the dog's diet. On the other hand, if we present any one part of the team in quantities that are too far out of proportion to the other parts, we can have the same disastrous results. **Balancing all the parts** of a nutritional team **is the most important factor** for formulating a proper diet for any dog. The complete nutritional team for canine nutrition consists of solids and liquids. These can be broken down to include: protein, vitamins, minerals, trace minerals, enzymes, fiber, fatty acids, carbohydrates, bacteria, and water. Then each part of the complete nutritional team can be broken down into a team of its own.

The protein team:
Protein consists of building blocks called amino acids. It is the balance of ten specific amino acids that give dietary protein its bio-nutritive value. The ten *essential* amino acids are; Valine, Leucine, Isoeucine, Threonine, Methionine, Phenylalanine, Tryptophan, Histidine, Argine, and Lysine. All ten of these must be present within the protein for a dog to receive any use of the protein at all. Other amino acids that are considered *non essential* amino acids are; Alanine, Asparagine, Aspartic Acid, Cystine, Glutamic Acid, Glutamine, Glysine, Proline, Serine and Tyrosine. The *non-essential* amino acids can be produced by the dog (in vivo) and therefore are not required in the dog's bulk food intake. The *essential* amino acids are the ones that must be in their food.

The vitamin team:
There are three types of vitamins required for proper canine nutrition: The water soluble vitamins of B-1, B-2, B-6, B-12, niacin or niacinamide, biotin, folic acid, d-calcium pantothenate, and para amino benzoic acid; The fat soluble vitamins of A, D, and E; and those vitamins like C and K that can be produced by the dog (in vivo) and therefore are not required in the dog's bulk food intake. I also include the nutrients of choline and inositol within the B complex vitamin team. These two nutrients are not considered vitamins. However, they work directly with the water soluble B vitamins and are so closely related that I place them in the same team.

The mineral team:

The minerals essential for canine nutrition consist of Calcium, Phosphorus, Potassium, Sodium, Chloride, Magnesium, Manganese, Iron, Copper, Iodine, Selenium, and Zinc. The common practice of adding one team member (Calcium) to a dog's diet by pet owners often produces the best example of the danger of unbalancing a nutritional team. This practice provides quantities of calcium that are too far out of proportion to the other team members. There have been many studies done that show adding calcium without the proper balance of the rest of its team mates can deform the skeletal structure in puppies. These studies are those most often used by nutritionists working for dog food companies to show the dangers of supplementing their "balanced" all-breed dog food. This team is also directly linked to the vitamins that are fat soluble and the balance between these two teams is extremely important.

The trace mineral team:

This team is directly related to both the mineral and vitamin teams. The trace mineral team consists of; Cobalt, Molybdenum, Copper, Fluorine, Iron, Arsenic, Magnesium, Zinc, Chromium, and Manganese. As you can see, many trace minerals appear to be the same as those listed as minerals. The main difference between those with the same name but found in a different category is their molecular configuration. Due to the unique molecular configuration of trace minerals they are very fragile. For example; the simple stone grinding process of wheat flour can cause from 70% to 90% of the natural *trace mineral* Iron to be destroyed. However, the same process would have little effect on the *mineral* form of Iron.

The enzyme team:

The enzyme team consists of Lypase, Amylase, and Trypsin. The dog's Pancreas secretes these enzymes into the intestines where they perform their team functions. Enzymes, like the nonessential amino acids of proteins that are produced by the dog in vivo, are not required in a healthy dog's bulk food intake. However, when supplemental enzymes are required, it is very important that they are manufactured in such a manner as to be released in the proper place within the dog's digestive system. The pancreas secretes its digestive enzymes into the digestive system when the food has already been exposed to several other digestive processes. By the time the food is exposed to the enzymes, the teeth have torn the food into smaller size, the acids and bacteria of the digestive system have started their work on the food, and so forth.

Enzymes have very specific duties to perform, and as with all digestive functions, there is a proper time and place for each specific function. When supplemental enzymes are introduced into the digestive process in the wrong place, they can interfere with the functions of individual nutrients or other nutritional teams.

The fiber team:
The fiber team is one of those teams that is often overlooked. However, the work it performs plays a major function in canine nutrition. Fiber is responsible for slowing the food's movement throughout the digestive system, thus allowing each part of that system the time to perform its function properly. Also fiber and bacteria join in the dogs gut to produce vitamin K.

One important thing to consider with fiber is how it differs by source. A wild carnivore may add fiber to its diet by eating the bark of a tree or grasses such as wheat or oats. The major differences here would be that tree bark will not swell in the gut like oats. Oats can swell up to ten times in size when they come into contact with a **canine's** gastric juices. Note: swelling of fiber can cause a problem if there are large quantities of this fiber from the wrong source in the dog's dietary intake. The swelling can produce a bulk within the intestine, which can impact the system. On the other hand, some sources of fiber that do not swell, like that from tree bark, may not allow the proper growth of bacteria **in a dog's gut** for that dog's in vivo production of vitamin K. It is very important to match the fiber source in the dietary intake of a dog with sources found in the breed's native environment.

The fatty acid team:
There are three fatty acids a dog must have to be able to produce the arachidonic acids that its body requires. The three fatty acids are: Oleic Acid, Linolenic Acid, and Linoleic Acid. All three are found together in any natural source containing what is called the Alpha-Linolenate family. The classic symptom of a fatty acid deficiency is a dry and brittle coat. The breeds that produce skin oils also will require a different balance of this team than those breeds that do not produce skin oils. The fatty acid team should not be confused with "fat", which is more a source of nutritional carbohydrates. However, some types of animal fats do contain both carbohydrates and small amounts of the fatty acids. Vegetables and grains such as wheat bran, corn, linseed, or soy beans normally contain the highest concentrations of the Alpha-Linolenate family.

The carbohydrate team:
Carbohydrate requirements change at very specific times in a dog's life cycle and in times of stress or work. Canines cannot "carbohydrate stack" (store carbohydrates for energy) as humans can, but they turn carbohydrates from the dietary intake into instant energy. Puppies and geriatric dogs should receive much of their energy from high carbohydrate food rather than from high protein food. Dogs convert high carbohydrate food into energy in a short time after ingesting it. They will need to be fed more often during the day to maintain proper energy levels. Also, in the time of lactation, the bitch will turn some carbohydrates into a very special form of milk sugars for her puppies' energy requirements. Producing energy from dietary carbohydrates can be much easier on the dog's body than the process of producing energy from protein. Protein must be stored in muscle tissue and then withdrawn for conversion into energy.

The bacteria team:
Like fiber, bacteria is a part of canine nutrition too often taken for granted. A wild carnivore will often bury its kill, after eating the guts (high in bacteria content), to let the carcass rot prior to eating it. This rotting is nothing more than allowing bacteria to break down the muscle tissue to make it more digestible. The bacteria team also works very closely with the fiber team within the digestive system to develop and grow cultures. These cultures in turn produce vitamin K in the dog's gut. New research is now being done with bacteria to study its role in canine nutrition, and its importance is becoming more defined.

Note: Bacteria is found throughout the dog's digestive system. Bacteria in the mouth should not be removed by chemicals so that the dog will have sweet smelling breath. This is a human's cultural hang-up, and one that can cause dietary distress in canines by removing a very essential nutritional part from a dog's digestive process.

The water team:
Water is the most important nutrient team. Water comprises over 60% of a dog's body weight. Deprivation of water causes death faster than deprivation of any other nutrient. Water also works with ALL the other nutrient teams in the performance of their individual or collective functions. Water intake is normally in balance with water loss through the dog's urine, lungs, skin and feces. The loss of water through each method depends on factors such as activity levels, stress levels and the environmental temperatures. Water must be replaced continuously because the loss of water is continuous.

This means that the dog must always have access to water. However, not all water is the same. Well water from an area high in soil minerals also will be high in those minerals unless treated. Many cities treat their water supply with chemicals. Each city will use different chemicals and treatment processes depending upon the sources of their water. The end product called "water" may only be similar to "water" from another city for the mere fact it is a liquid. Dogs can develop diarrhea from a sudden change in the sources of any nutrient and water is no exception. Therefore, I recommend you try to provide water from the home source when traveling with a dog. This can be done by taking along water from home or you can acclimate your dog to a specific type of bottled water before the trip. Then all you need to do is buy the same type of bottled water as needed during the trip.

There are dangers in breaking down nutritional teams of solid food and liquids into their component parts and in turn further breaking down each of these components. One danger is that a person doing research in the field of nutrition can become too focused on a specific nutrient and disregard how that one nutrient interacts with other nutrients. For example; we all know that it takes calcium to build heathy bones. Knowing this *one fact* and taking it out of context can lead to problems. Adding lots of calcium to a puppy's food, without the other nutrients calcium interacts with for building bones, can be counter productive. Another danger occurs when the researcher is looking for a specific result. When the researcher achieves his goal, he does not carry on to see what other areas have been effected. The best example of this would be the research on a product to change the elasticity of the muscles holding the hip joint together, thus changing the occurrence of hip dysplasia. Such a product has been researched and is available. However, that product also damages an otherwise healthy dog's liver and kidney.

When considering the field of canine nutrition and formulating a proper diet for your dog, I feel that a holistic view must be taken.

Therefore, again I will emphasize that I feel **the balancing of *all the parts* of each nutritional team is the most important factor.**

Each breed of dog has
physical or temperamental characteristics
that are different from any other breed.

The question is
NOT IF *those characteristics affect*
a breed's nutritional requirements,
BUT HOW MUCH *do they affect a*
breed's nutritional requirements?

WE SHOULD KNOW:
A thick boned breed of dog
will need different amounts
of the bone building minerals
than a thin boned breed of dog

PROTEIN
AND ITS AMINO ACIDS

Protein is one of the most important parts of dog food, as well as one of the least understood by the average dog owner. Most people have the misconception that the amount of protein the food contains is the important factor. However, the important factor is: *How much of the food's protein can be used by the animal consuming it?* To determine the amount of usable protein, we must first break protein down into its component parts. These parts are called amino acids. There are two classifications for amino acids of dietary protein; (1) essential - those that the dog's own body *cannot* manufacture in sufficient quantities and (2) non essential - those that the dog's own body *can* manufacture in sufficient quantities. It is the presence, balance and quality of the essential amino acids that determines the bio-nutritive value (% of usable protein) of the protein in a dog's feeding program.

All the amino acids, both essential and non-essential, have very specific nutritional jobs within the dog's body; such as the building of the muscle tissue, the regulation of antibodies within the immune system, and the transfer of nerve impulses etc.

The essential amino acids and some of their functions for a dog are:

ARGININE: This essential amino acid stimulates immune system response by enhancing the production of T-cells, has a protective effect of toxicity of hydrocarbons and intravenous diuretics, is related to the elevated ammonia levels and cirrhosis of the liver by detoxifying ammonia, and induces growth hormone release from the pituitary gland.

HISTIDINE: This essential amino acid releases histamines from body stores, is associated with pain control, is associated with arthritis, and widens small blood vessels; thus aiding early digestion by stimulating stomach acid secretion.

ISOLEUCINE and LEUCINE: see VALINE

LYSINE: This essential amino acid promotes bone growth in puppies, stimulates secretion of gastric juices, and is found in abundance within muscle tissue, connective tissue, and collagen.

15

METHIONINE: This essential amino acid assists gall bladder functions by participating in the synthesis of blue salts, helps to prevent deposits and cohesion of fats in the liver due to lipotropic function, is related to the synthesis of choline, balances the urinary tract pH (in its dl form), and gives rise to Taurine (an important neuroregulator in the brain).

PHENYALANINE: This essential amino acid stimulates chaleceptokinin enzymes and thus is related to appetite control, increases blood pressure in hypotension, works with minerals in skin and hair pigmentation, gives rise to Tyrosine, and produces adrenaline and noreadrenaline.

THREONINE: This essential amino acid regulates energy draw requirements, works with Phenylalanine in mood elevation or depression and skin pigmentation, manufactures adrenaline, and precurses Thyroid hormone.

TRYPTOPHAN: This essential amino acid produces Serotonin that induces sleep, precurses the vitamin Niacin in treating and preventing pellagra, and is a vasoconstrictor that appears to aid in blood clotting mechanisms. Studies indicate a lack of tryptophan and methionine together can cause hair loss.

VALINE, (ISOLEUCINE AND LEUCINE): These essential amino acids work together and are classified as "branched-chain" amino acids. The three combine to regulate the protein turnover and energy metabolism, are stored in muscle tissue, and are released to be converted into energy during times of fasting or between meals.

Listed above are the ten amino acids that are essential for a dog's dietary requirements. Note humans only require eight essential amino acids in our dietary intake, and for this reason a dog could starve if given the same protein sufficient to sustain human life.

Other factors to consider concerning a specific dog's protein requirements are:
  (1) The age of a dog can change its protein requirements. Both puppies and geriatric dogs require lower amounts of protein and higher carbohydrate %'s in their food.
  (2) The dog's activity level or stress level (due to environment or working conditions) can change its protein requirements.
  (3) A bitch during the gestation and lactation period has her own very specific requirements.

(4) The other ingredients within the food can affect the amount of each amino acid required. For example, a food that is highly acidic (due to a preservative) can increase the requirement of the amino acid Methionine.

The problem of selecting the proper protein blend for a specific dog can be very confusing but can be simplified by applying this single rule: *When choosing the protein blend that is best for a specific breed of dog look for the protein sources that were in that specific breed's native environment and then match them as closely as possible.*

When considering an environment's protein sources you should take many factors into consideration. First, with the environment's meat protein sources you should remember to look beyond labels such as *cattle* before assuming that they are describing beef. In some parts of the world the term *cattle* can be referring to a herd of goats, water buffalos, or reindeer. *Cattle* may not always mean beef from the state of Texas. Also with each protein source the amino acid balance can be different depending upon the environment from which we take our sample. When testing food sources, we find that *herring* from the Pacific Ocean has a different amino acid profile than *herring* from the Atlantic Ocean. Also, Texas longhorn cattle produces *beef* with a different amino acid profile than Pennsylvania dairy cattle *beef.*

Second, consider **all** the protein sources of the area to establish if that environment's meat protein is the type of protein that is best for a specific breed. For example; The Chow Chow developed in an area of China where meat is available as a dietary source of protein. However, the meat source of protein was the Chow Chow and it was available to the humans. The Chow was fed grains to produce a tender and nicely marbled meat for the human's table. This breed's development as a vegetarian also explains why today's Chow Chow has the jaw and flat tooth structure of a grain eater. Also, why today's Chow Chow has a body with a high fat to low muscle fiber ratio. Therefore, after considering all the factors for a Chow Chow's dietary protein, it may be best to use only the vegetable sources of protein found in its native environment.

Third, the amount of each protein source used in a single dog food becomes important since the amount of each source found in a specific environment can be quite different. A breed that developed in an environment that had few grain crops would need less grain in their food

17

than a breed that developed in an area where grain protein comprised the bulk of their dietary protein intake.

Fourth, the blend of protein sources is important since different sources of dietary protein contain different amounts of both the essential and non-essential amino acids. For example, equal amounts of lamb meat, beef, fish, chicken, or horse meat from the same environment will contain different amounts of essential amino acids. Sources such as soy, corn, rice, beet, wheat, and alfalfa also contain very specific amounts of essential and non-essential amino acids in their protein.

The following two tables show how different protein food sources can provide different amounts or types of protein.

Table P-1: The differences in protein and fat ratios of different meat sources from different areas of the world.

Food source:	% of Protein	Protein to Fat ratio
Domesticated Pig	12.5 %	1 to 3
Wild Warthog	13.0 %	10 to 1
Western Domesticated Beef	11.6 %	1 to 3
Western Wild Venison	14.0 %	7 to 1
East African Eland	12.0 %	6 to 1
East African Buffalo	15.0 %	5 to 1

Table P-2: The following table shows relative comparisons for amino acid amounts of some common commercial dog food protein sources.

Food source (100 g. each)	Arg	Cys	His	Iso	Leu	Lys	Met	Phe	Thr	Try	Tyr	Val
Chicken	1378	311	655	1125	1653	1765	591	899	922	257	732	1100
Turkey	1979	308	845	1409	2184	2557	790	1100	1227	311	1066	1464
Beef	-	-	-	1329	2081	2220	631	1045	1122	297	-	1411
Lamb	-	-	-	1068	1595	1667	494	837	943	267	-	1015
Pork	-	-	-	1510	2164	2414	733	1157	1364	382	-	1529
Soybeans	-	-	-	649	935	759	165	594	423	165	-	638
Tuna	1518	-	1619	1316	2024	2327	810	1012	1214	-	303	1417
Herring (Atl)	-	-	-	882	1315	1522	502	640	761	173	-	934
Herring (Pac)	-	-	-	892	1312	1522	508	648	752	175	-	928

Note: the above table compares meat to meat,
not to a meal or by-product source.

FAT CARBOHYDRATES
AND
FATTY ACIDS

There are differences between the dog and human in their use of carbohydrates. This includes the use of different forms of carbohydrates from starch or sugar. For example; we know sugar forms of lactose, dextrose or glucose are all different as dietary sources of carbohydrates. These can be stored or used as an instant energy supply by a human. Also, we know how a human stores carbohydrates from some starch sources better than sugar sources for future energy requirements. Only the human can store dietary carbohydrates for later conversion into energy. Canines turn all dietary carbohydrates, from any source, into instant energy, and none is stored for energy requirements that develop later. Also, **for all types of dogs, all forms of sugar carbohydrates have been found to be detrimental**, except for lactose found in the milk of a lactating bitch for *her* puppy. *Please Note; this form of lactose is not the same as a synthetic lactose from sugar beet or sugar cane or even the lactose found in the milk of other species of mammals.*

Like the sugar carbohydrates of lactose, glucose and dextrose being different, carbohydrates found in animal fat, vegetable and grain sources (soy bean, beet pulp, wheat, rice, potatoes or corn) are all different. These differences are important. One study cited in the NRC publication <u>Nutrient Requirements of Dogs</u> shows that the digestible fat from one source provides 2.25 times the metabolizable energy concentration of digestible carbohydrate than from a second source. Another study cited showed different breeds of dog need different amounts of carbohydrates or different carbohydrate to protein ratios in their food. Therefore, if your dog is requiring a high carbohydrate diet due to breed requirements or life-style, you need to provide those carbohydrates in the proper amount and from the proper source.

When you are considering which food source of carbohydrates contains the proper form for your dog, you should consider the type of food sources that were in the native environment for your breed. Then also remember to eliminate those sources that would have been foreign to that breed's native environment. A dog breed from Ireland, where potatoes or flax were common dietary sources of carbohydrates, would not have been exposed to rice.

Yet a dog breed from China could have been exposed to several different types of rice that were grown as common sources of dietary carbohydrates in its environment. A dog breed from a mountain environment, where both vegetable and grain crops are scarce, could have a different need for its carbohydrate source as well. Some mountain breeds of dog may not utilize potato or rice carbohydrate any better than a sugar, but best use an animal fat form of carbohydrate.

Animal fat is one of the most common carbohydrate sources found in commercial dog food and because a food contains animal fat, it is often assumed it is providing dietary fatty acids. Normally this is not so since animal fat in dog food is exposed to extremely high temperatures during processing procedures. The high temperature can eliminate the polyunsaturated fatty acid content of the rendered fat. In many cases manufacturers use separate food sources to provide fat carbohydrates and polyunsaturated fatty acids in their foods. The better commercial dog food manufacturers use grain or vegetable oils that have been cold pressed or processed to retain the needed polyunsaturated fatty acids. These cold pressed grain and vegetable oils still contain the fatty acids known as the alpha-linolenate family. There are three fatty acids that make up the entire alpha-linolenate family; oleic acid, linolenic acid, and linoleic acid. With breeds that produce skin oil, the requirement for the oleic acid part of the alpha-linolenate family is higher than with the breeds that do not produce skin oils. However, it is essential for all dogs to receive all three of these fatty acids to produce the arachidonic acids they all require. Since these fatty acids are a complete nutritional team, they should be listed on labels in the same way that manufacturers of premium foods list the amino acid content of their food's protein. Manufacturers who list all three on the label provide you with a more accurate statement of the package contents. This labeling practice enables you to choose more intelligently the proper food for your specific breed of dog.

In processed dog foods animal fat should be considered as only a source of dietary carbohydrates. After the rendering process, it contains very little of the alpha-linolenate fatty acids. A complete diet for most breeds of dog should contain both animal fat and a source containing the alpha-linolenate family of polyunsaturated fatty acids. Do not assume fatty acids are present just because the dog food label has fat listed. The finished product may or may not have any fatty acids. Commercial food manufacturers may add animal fat just for its carbohydrate content or to make it more palatable for most canines.

Also do not assume that the product contains all three of the fatty acids of the alpha-linolenate family if the label only lists Linoleic acid. This one fatty acid can be purchased separately as a raw material for dog food.

Table F-1: The following table shows relative comparisons for some common commercial dog food fat and fatty acid sources.

| Food source | alpha-linolenate Fatty Acids | | |
	oleic acid	linolenic acid	linoleic acid
Rendered Chicken fat	under 0.1%	under 0.1%	under 0.1%
Rendered Beef fat	under 0.1%	under 0.1%	under 0.1%
Rendered Pork fat	under 0.1%	under 0.1%	under 0.1%
Cold pressed Linseed oil	36%	11.4%	42.5%
Cold pressed Wheat germ oil	30%	10.8%	44.1%
Cold pressed Soy bean oil	26%	11.0%	49.0%

Both carbohydrates and fatty acids are important and both must be provided in dog foods. However, you must use a source of carbohydrates or fatty acids that can be assimilated by the breed of dog you are feeding.

An indicator that your dog is rejecting food carbohydrates from sugar, grains, vegetables or animal fat in the food is persistent diarrhea. The indicator that your dog is not assimilating the fatty acids is a loss of coat shine or a loss in the skin's elasticity. Therefore, it is easy for the dog owner to see a dietary carbohydrate or fatty acid nutritional problem. Conversely, it is also easy to see when foods are supplying the proper sources and amounts of these important nutrients.

Each breed of dog has
physical or temperamental characteristics
that are different from any other breed.

The question is
NOT IF *those characteristics affect*
a breed's nutritional requirements,
BUT HOW MUCH *do they affect a*
breed's nutritional requirements?

WE SHOULD KNOW:
A black / thick / long / double coat will filter out
the sun's ultraviolet light
differently than a white / thin / short / single coat.

&

Because the sun's ultraviolet light
manufactures vitamin D on a dog's skin
that different breeds can have
different requirements for this one nutrient.

INDIVIDUAL FUNCTIONS OF VITAMINS & MINERALS

Vitamin A Important for healthy skin, hair, eyes, and normal bone growth.

Vitamin B-1 Essential in the metabolism of carbohydrates and protein. Deficiency causes heart and nerve disease.

Vitamin B-2 Essential for normal growth, healthy skin and hair. It has been used as a natural aid in coping with stress.

Vitamin B-6 Essential for normal blood, nerves and growth, and metabolism of protein.

Vitamin B-12 Important in the development and maintenance of normal blood cells.

Vitamin D Needed to assimilate the calcium and phosphorous in the development of normal teeth and bones.

Vitamin E Protects against effects of oxidized or unstable fats in diet. It is important for reproduction and helps the body use Vitamin A.

Niacinamide Helps to maintain the integrity of mouth tissue and the nervous system and is essential in converting food to energy.

Biotin Present as a member of the B Complex in nature and is associated with normal growth, healthy skin and hair.

Folic Acid A hematopoietic vitamin, used for normal blood, growth and health of the fetus.

d-Calcium Pantothenate Required for the formation of certain hormones and nerve-regulating substances and to maintain the proper level of blood sugars.

Para Amino Benzoic Acid Helps the body use proteins, fats, and carbohydrates. It is important in the body's rejection of infection.

Selenium Interacts with Vitamin E and is associated with normal liver, muscle, and reproductive function.

Lecithin Significant constituent of nervous tissue and brain substance. It also breaks down cholesterol and prevents fatty infiltration of the heart and liver.

Calcium Essential for formation of normal teeth and bones and is important in the transmission of nerve impulses, and muscle contraction.

Copper Works within the digestive system for normal iron use and maintenance of normal bones and hair.

Iodine Necessary for normal thyroid function and works with protein to form thyroxines in the thyroid gland.

Iron Important to the transfer of oxygen in blood and muscles and is essential to the development and maintenance of normal red blood cells.

Magnesium Necessary for normal tooth and bone formation and is important to cellular energy transfer and normal muscle and heart function.

Manganese Assists magnesium and other minerals in the formation of normal teeth and bones.

Phosphorus Essential to storage and release of energy in blood cells. It must be present for formation of normal teeth and bones.

Potassium Necessary for normal body growth, fluid balance, and muscle contraction.

Zinc Essential constituent of insulin and is necessary for normal growth and healthy skin and hair.

Note: Please do not take the information in this one chapter out of the context of the book. Remember that each of these nutrients is a team member and should be provided in balance with the other team nutrients as outlined in the chapter on "Nutritional Teamwork."

SUPPLEMENTING

Webster's New World Dictionary defines **supplement:** (sup. ple. ment) as: *something added, esp. to make up for a lack or deficiency.*

Supplementing is a two edged sword; there is good supplementing and there is bad supplementing.

All dog food manufacturers add various ingredients to their foods during the manufacturing process so that the end product contains levels that meet industry standards. For example, to make protein that dogs can use the manufacturer may add various protein sources that have one or more of the essential amino acids. They do this until they have a protein blend that contains all ten essential amino acids. Thus, by the process defined as supplementing, the dog food company manufactures a food that will have nutritional value. The same supplementing is done to achieve nutritional levels of vitamins, minerals and other ingredients in all commercially manufactured dog food. Most foods are brought to levels that have been established by the government National Research Council (NRC) as the Minimum Nutrient Requirements of Dogs. When dog food companies have added ingredients to reach NRC recommended levels, they have also reached the industry standards to advertise the food as "complete and balanced."

These NRC or "complete and balanced" levels are also **established to provide safe levels** for **all** dogs. For example, the NRC subcommittee recommends that dog foods supply 8 IU of vitamin D per kilogram of a dog's body weight. This is 8 IU/kg. for any breed of dog's body weight, even though tests cited in a NRC publication show that some breeds require higher amounts of vitamin D (up to 270 IU/kg.). Since vitamin D is a "fat soluble" vitamin, **overdoses of this vitamin are dangerous**. If manufacturers added enough vitamin D to meet the higher requirements of the few breeds that require 270 IU/kg., the food would actually be toxic to the many breeds who only require 8 IU/kg.

The dog food companies take care to not exceed the safe all-breed levels of any nutrient that could be harmful to a breed. They have no control over which breed of dog will consume their food.

Many studies show that any supplementing of a single nutrient to safe "complete and balanced" dog food levels can be dangerous.

Some examples are:
   A) Excess supplemental calcium can block the assimilation of the copper, iron, phosphorus and zinc in the dietary intake.
   B) Excess supplemental vitamin A (a fat soluble vitamin) can decalcify the teeth and bones and cause liver damage.
   C) Any supplemental vitamin C can cause a detrimental pH change in the kidney and cause a healthy liver to lose its ability to function properly.
   D) Excess supplemental vitamin D (a fat soluble vitamin) can block calcium assimilation or collect in the glands to levels that can be toxic.
   E) Any supplemental fluoride or fluorine can mottle tooth enamel during the period of calcification of permanent teeth in dogs. It also can block the assimilation of dietary trace minerals and alter the dog's natural ability to produce vitamin K.
   F) Any supplemental thyroid can cause a healthy thyroid gland to lose its ability to function properly.

Supplementing can be dangerous when any one nutrient is added in quantities that negatively affect how the dog's body reacts to the other nutrients in the same nutritional complex, or when by supplementing we change or take over the function of a vital organ.

To avoid potential dangers, most dog food companies make a blanket recommendation that you do not supplement their foods.

When dog food companies recommend that you do not supplement their food, they are correct . . . *about 50% correct!*

What they haven't told you is that there is another side to the issue. The side that shows that the safe all-breed levels they have in their all-breed foods are not sufficient nutritional amounts for all dogs. The safe all-breed amounts may be enough to keep any dog alive. But the safe all-breed amounts will not provide the correct amounts or balance to sustain optimum health for some breeds of dogs. *All-breed foods, even though they contain nutritional levels that allow them to be classified by* **industry standards** *as "complete and balanced" also must be supplemented above these levels to provide proper nutrition for most dogs.*

Dog owners may recognize their animals are not in the optimum of health because the all-breed foods they are using are lacking the proper nutrient amounts for their dogs. Then with the best intentions, they may choose to ignore the dog food companies' recommendations about supplementing and experiment with their dogs dietary intake. Experimenting with supplements usually produces negative, or at best, limited results.

Supplementing dog food is a complicated process. It is possible to do it correctly at the time of manufacturing, if the manufacturer is making a breed specific food.

There is only one way that dog foods should be supplemented during the manufacturing process:

Step one is to calculate the nutritional requirements of the specific breed of dog that will be eating that food.

Step two is to determine which sources of each nutrient have the proper molecular formation for that breed of dog to assimilate.

Step three is to find food bases with these sources.

Step four is to acquire quantities of the nutrients from the proper sources.

Step five is to blend the proper amount of each of these nutrients to bring the levels and balances in the finished food to the proper levels and balances for that specific breed of dog's requirements.

It is also possible to supplement a pre-manufactured all-breed formula correctly.

Step one is to calculate the nutritional requirements of the specific breed of dog involved.

Step two is to determine which sources of each nutrient have the proper molecular formation for this breed of dog to assimilate.

Step three is to find a pre-manufactured all-breed formula with these sources.

Step four is to analyze the bulk food to determine what levels are already present.

Step five is to acquire quantities of the additional nutrients needed (these also must be from the proper sources).

Step six is to blend the proper amount of each of these additional nutrients to bring the levels and balances in the final food blend to the proper levels and balances for that specific breed of dog's requirements.

But here I caution you: *Do not compound the problems that now exist in feeding a safe but nutritionally inadequate all-breed dog food by supplementing it with an unsafe or imbalanced all-breed supplement.*

NUTRIENTS BENEFICIAL TO HUMANS ... *BUT* ... HARMFUL TO DOGS

There are many nutritional similarities between a dog and a human, but we also have many differences. The human has an average of 32 permanent teeth (with structural differences depending on the race). The dog has an average of 42 permanent teeth (with structural differences depending on the breed). The human has a long gastrointestinal tract consisting of both a large and a small intestine. The dog has a short gastrointestinal tract consisting of a single colon. Similar glands found within both humans and canines are located differently within their respective digestive systems and some glands, such as the liver, perform different functions. The human has starch breaking enzymes in the saliva, the dog does not. The human can store carbohydrates for energy, the dog cannot. The human can receive bio-nutritive value from protein containing 8 essential amino acids, the dog requires 10 essential amino acids to receive bio-nutritive value. A stimulant in chocolate called theobromine can be deadly for dogs but not for humans. Etc.

Because of the differences, there are certain nutrients beneficial when they are in a human's dietary intake that can be harmful in a dog's dietary intake. Two of the most common nutrients I have found in commercial canine dietary products that fall into this category are Fluorine and Vitamin C.

Fluorine:
Fluorine, as sodium fluoride, was added to the water of most commercial sources within the U.S. after extensive research showed that it hardened the tooth enamel in children and thus helped to prevent tooth decay. However, the same type of research has been performed on the dog, with the results being quite different. To find some research with fluorine and canines we need to look into the history books. In 1936 (Biester et. al.) conducted research showing that the addition of fluorine to the water supply of canines caused mottling of the tooth enamel during the period of calcification of the permanent teeth. In 1959 (Andreeva) reported findings that the addition of fluorine at 20 milligrams per kilogram of body weight daily for 92 days to the diet of month-old pups altered serum calcium and inorganic and organic phosphorus concentrations significantly.

There are many other tests that show fluorine can cause many nutritionally related problems. Fluorine should not be included within the dietary intake of any breed of dog.

Therefore, I suggest that you filter the dog's water supply to eliminate the fluorine. This can be done by adding an inexpensive filter to the water supply for the kennel. By properly locating the filter you can remove the fluorine from the dog's water while leaving the fluorine in the main water supply to meet the human's needs.

Vitamin C:
Vitamin C is an essential nutrient for all mankind. However, one of the most common errors when looking at this one vitamin is to think that all vitamin C is the same. Often vitamin C is referred to as ascorbic acid, or vice versa, even though **ascorbic acid is only one form of vitamin C.** Ascorbic acid is the most common synthetic form used in the U. S. and is also found in both a "L" and a "D" form. Since the "D" form is unsafe for human use, only the "L" form is sold commercially. L. Pauling in his book <u>VITAMIN C AND THE COMMON COLD</u> discusses both the "L" and "D" forms of ascorbic acid. <u>THE MERCK INDEX</u>, an encyclopedia of chemicals and drugs, also lists these two forms

The three most common synthetic forms of vitamin C sold in the U. S. are Ascorbic Acid (**C6H8O6**), Calcium Ascorbate (**C12H14CaO12**), and Sodium Ascorbate (**C6H7NaO6**). Note that the molecular forms within the ( )'s are all different. In addition, none of these forms are the same as the natural vitamin C found in fresh fruit. They also differ from the vitamin C that a dog and certain other animals can manufacture within their glandular systems.

Another common error associated with vitamin C is to assume that the human and the dog are both the same in their dietary need of this nutrient. A very basic difference between dogs and humans is found in their glandular systems. Using the trace mineral form of Cobalt as the primary element, when all the other trace minerals are present within their diet, **the dog's liver has the ability to synthesize the cobalt to produce the vitamin C that its body requires.** The human glandular system is not capable of producing its own vitamin C. For this reason, it is **essential for humans**, *but not dogs*, to include vitamin C in their dietary intake.

As an interesting side light I note: The source of the vitamin C that a human should use in their dietary intake also can be an important factor. A recent study conducted by the University of Oregon (1987), discovered that the American Eskimo people are unable to use the synthetic forms of vitamin C. This includes ascorbic acid, or even those natural forms found in fresh fruit to prevent the onset of scurvy. However, they are able to prevent scurvy by eating seal blubber that contains a special and unique molecular form of vitamin C. The seal produces this form of vitamin C in much the same way that a dog does by synthesizing trace minerals in the liver. The seal then stores this "fat soluble" form of vitamin C in the blubber, just under the skin. This fat soluble form, which is stored in seal blubber, is also different in its molecular structure than ascorbil palmitate, a commercial synthetic "fat soluble" vitamin C.

Research done with dogs documenting their vitamin C requirements is readily available. For example, the government has published the results from research projects with vitamin C in their 1985 revision of the NRC NUTRIENT REQUIREMENTS OF DOGS. On pages 37 and 38 of the NRC publication they cite twenty five **carefully controlled studies.** An excerpt says: "and some veterinary practitioners apparently advocate vitamin C for - - -", and continues "- - - conducted some carefully controlled studies concerned with these issues and established that exogenous vitamin C was of no benefit. " One controlled study cited in the NRC showed that supplemental vitamin C aggravated skeletal disease in Labrador Retriever puppies. From these **controlled studies** the government subcommittee on animal nutrition states: *"It is concluded that there is no adequate evidence to justify recommendation of routine vitamin C additions to the diet of the normal dog."*

Other studies have shown that supplemental vitamin C from the ascorbic acid source can create a pH imbalance in the dog's kidney. This is due to ascorbic **acid**, which is "water soluble", being discharged through the kidney. These studies also show where this change in the urinary tract pH can negatively affect the use of many other essential nutrients.

Another negative aspect of giving vitamin C to a healthy dog is the risk taken when we replace one of the functions of a healthy dog's liver (producing the vitamin C that its own body requires).

By adding vitamin C to the dog's diet we can cause the dog's liver to stop working as it should. This can best be equated to feeding thyroid medication to a dog with a normal thyroid gland.

The Morris Animal Foundation in 1987 released the findings of a survey determining the main causes of dogs' deaths in the United States. The second and sixth leading causes cited in that report were kidney disorders and liver failure. I cannot help but wonder at the connection between these statistics and the use of ascorbic acid in dog food or dog food supplements.

Even after all the negative test results cited by the National Research Council, many dog food manufacturers still add ascorbic acid to their dog foods. These test results have been confirmed by companies within the dog food industry itself. One company; Gains Pet Food Corp., has published a book titled BASIC GUIDE TO CANINE NUTRITION. On page 21 in their fifth edition of that book they state: "Vitamin C (ascorbic acid) is not required in the diet of dogs as it is in the diets of primates, guinea pigs, bats and some fish, birds, and insects. The dog and other animals are able to synthesize this vitamin."

Why do many dog food manufacturers have ascorbic acid in their foods? The reason is ascorbic acid is an antioxidant. As an antioxidant, ascorbic acid is a commonly used cheap preservative that has been used for years to keep foods fresh, color additives bright, and to keep the fats within the foods from going rancid. It is a cheap preservative that most *people* can assimilate. Therefore, people formulating dog foods, who do not know there is a nutritional difference between dogs and humans, *assume* it to be a "safe" preservative. The other scenario is that it is being used by people formulating dog foods who are aware of the harm it can do. But these people are more concerned about keeping the colors in their food bright and appealing for the buyer, rather than the actual health of the dogs that are eating it.

Manufacturers of commercial dog foods must remember that when formulating a food for dogs, **the finished food product is for a dog and not for human consumption.** The dog and the human are two different species of animal. We may have similarities, but we also have our differences. Therefore, the food should provide the nutrients that a dog requires and should not contain nutrients that can be detrimental to the animal for which it is formulated.

TRUSTING LABELS

Buyer Beware! You could be feeding your dog poultry feathers or sawdust. These ingredients are often listed on a label so that you think you are getting real chunks of poultry meat or beef. Most dog food labels can be confusing or misleading to the average lay person, though the labels may be technically correct by government standards.

When you consider the competitive dog food market in the U.S.A., you can see why the manufacturers want to have the most appealing packaging possible. They also need to formulate their products to be price competitive. To do this, many manufacturers buy their ingredients from the cheapest source - not necessarily the best source. Most cheaper sources used are "feed grade" or "animal grade" food products. Feed grade products commonly used in commercial dog foods are corn husk, peanut shells, oat middlings, poultry feathers, sawdust and fish heads with skin. These have their own set of government label requirements. Unless you are familiar with the government list of feed grade products and their labeling requirements, odds are you will be confused or even misled by the label terms used. Much of the confusion is because there are nutritional products made for human consumption, from high quality ingredients, that have similar sounding labeling terms. When we read a label on food products for an animal we *assume* that if it sounds the same it must be the same. NOT SO!

For example, when dog food labels show protein as an ingredient, we may *assume* that the protein has food value equal to the percentage of protein listed. However, not all protein is nutritionally usable protein. It is protein! Protein that can be shown on the label because it can be determined by a simple nitrogen analysis. Both the federal government and dog food industry use this analysis to confirm the label claim for protein. But according to this nitrogen analysis, the plastic of your telephone or the paint on your wall also contains protein. As far fetched as it sounds, these protein sources could be used in dog food and the food could be sold as a "High Protein Food." NOTE: *Present labeling laws for dog foods require that they show the amount of protein content. The requirements do not ask for a break down of the protein for its amino acid content or its bio-nutritive value.* Many low food value - high protein feed grade sources are used in commercial dog foods. Often they are listed on the label as a "*meal* " or "*by-products* ."

Webster defines **by-product** as: *anything produced in the course of making another thing; secondary or incidental product or result.*

The production of meat for human consumption also produces *meat meal* and *meat by-products* used in dog food. **It is important to note that there is not necessarily any meat in the products that are put into dog food and labeled as a "by-product",** there also may be very little meat in the product labeled as *"meal."*

For example, when the slaughter house scrapes the hair and viscera from the hide before sending it to be tanned for leather products, they save this for dog foods that use meat *by-products.* Another meat *by-product* is sawdust from the floor of the packing house. The sawdust on the floors of a butchering plant catches the blood and viscera during the butchering process and keeps the floors from getting slippery. Therefore, the blood soaked sawdust has become a *meat by-product.* **The *by-product* of poultry meat production is feathers.** On pages 48 through 61 of the NRC's 1985 publication Nutrient Requirements of Dogs there is a list of ingredients found in dog food, including their international feed numbers. For example on page 60 under Poultry, entries 109-111: feathers, hydrolyzed (international feed number 5-03-795) can be listed on a label as *Poultry by-product* ; necks with backs and wings with legs, fresh (international feed number 5-03-797) can be listed on a label as *Poultry meal* ; trimmings fresh (international feed number 5-16-424) can be listed on a label as *Poultry* or *Poultry meat* .

Obviously, *Poultry meat* is what we want and what we hope we are getting when reading a dog food label listing poultry as a food source. However, you should remember to read the entire listing. If the word *by-product* is used the food is just that - *a by-product* !

Food product manufacturers who are meeting government labeling regulations must list the ingredients on product labels showing what the product contains. This is done under a heading entitled *Guaranteed Analysis* or *Ingredients* on the label. Yet representatives for dog food manufacturers have often told me that the food they make contains real poultry meat though the label states that it contains *Poultry by-products.* Government agencies check the printed label. If they lie on the label the government can take the product off the market shelves. Therefore, I suggest that we trust the printed word more than a sales representative's claims.

Most dog food manufacturers would not label their product showing a *by-product* food source if they could show the product was made with a source that was better. **Remember that the dog food manufacturer, in most cases, is meeting the federal label law requirements.**

Also remember that when buying a dog food product it is "buyer beware." It is your responsibility to know how to look beyond a fancy ad or the misleading name on the front of the package. It is up to you to know that "meaty flavored" or "looks just like real meat" does not mean there is any meat in the product.

Most dog food manufacturers also use the MISLEADING CLAIM that their dog food is "complete and balanced." The claim "complete and balanced" means that the manufacturer has met certain all-breed minimums or industry standards. The claim of "complete and balanced" means that the food contains the *complete number* and *balance of nutrients* the government suggested dog food should have as a minimum. The claim of "complete and balanced" **does not mean** that a food is *nutritionally complete* or *nutritionally balanced* **for the requirements of the dog that is eating it.**

If you have any questions about your specific dog and the food it is eating you should be able to ask the dog food manufacturer. There is a way to do this:

For the consumer's protection the federal label laws require that manufacturers of food products include on their label the name and postal zip code of the manufacturer or responsible distributor. The company listed on the label also must maintain a listed telephone number in the area that corresponds to the postal zip code on the label. There must be a responsible person available at that number to answer any questions that a government inspector would want to ask. This is the person you should talk to, not just a sales person or receptionist. When you get through to this person **do not accept a long answer that doesn't tell you anything. Ask questions that can be answered by a** *yes* **or** *no* **and demand clear concise answers.**

For example, "Does your product contain sugar?" can be answered by a simple yes or no. Yet when I asked that question to the person in charge of Quality Control for a manufacturer of a well known dog food supplement, I was told: "If you tested our products you could find traces of carbohydrates."

The fact was, when tested, their product was 92% sugar. However, the sugar in this product is considered a "filler." The government label regulations do not require this "filler" to be listed. Therefore, it was *legally* not shown on their label.

Also, we bought this product from a veterinary clinic. Which brings me to another touchy subject; **Who can you trust to give you good information based on KNOWLEDGE?**

An alarming fact is canine nutrition is not adequately covered in the curriculum of most schools of veterinary medicine. A recent survey showed that the average school of veterinary medicine in the United States donated approximately five classroom hours, one hour per day for five day's, on all-animal nutrition in their curriculum requirements to obtain a D. V. M.. There are exceptions, so here again, **you should ask *where and how*** the person giving you nutritional advice gained their knowledge. If they gained their knowledge by attending seminars put on by dog food companies, and they are selling that brand of dog food, then it is BUYER BEWARE. However, if they are among the conscientious veterinarians who have taken it upon themselves to study animal nutrition from an unbiased source, you have found a gem.

When you are asking for nutritional information about a product *from anyone*, **consider if the person you are asking is trying to make money by selling you a product.** Then consider if they may be biassing the information that they are giving you.

Trust the PRINTED word
                    BUT
                              READ THE ENTIRE LABEL!

DO NOT ASSUME! . . . . . . .ASK!

IT IS UP TO YOU TO FIND OUT!

THE RESPONSIBILITY BELONGS TO NOBODY ELSE!

YOU CAN ONLY TRUST YOURSELF!

LABEL WORDING DEFINITIONS

One pet food company advertises their food as better than a cheaper food because the main ingredient in their food is poultry meat and (according to the ad) the cheaper foods are made with feathers. But when we read the labels on all the different pet foods we can't find "feathers" listed as an ingredient in any of them. The company advertising their food is made with poultry meat even has the same ingredients listed on their label as those cheaper foods. Who are we to trust? The words used on pet food labels can hide many evils. They are sometimes misunderstood, often ignored and can be confusing. To limit confusion when listing each ingredient in a food, all pet food companies should be required to also use the International Feed Number (IFN) that has been assigned to each feed grade ingredient. Then we could clearly identify the ingredients in each pet food and be able to make intelligent choices amongst them.

Today, words used in the ingredient list can be hiding what is really in the food. Things like feathers, sawdust and dehydrated pig excreta all have IFN's that would identify them. Current regulations allow ingredients like these to be put in pet food and labeled with wording so you don't know they are in there."

To help you determine what may be in the pet food you are now buying, here are definitions of some words that can be found on most pet food labels today:

By-product:
    An ingredient produced in the course of making a primary food ingredient; a secondary or incidental product. Feathers are a by-product of poultry meat processing. Feathers which are removed from a carcass during production of poultry meat are then hydrolyzed (pressure cooked with steam until they are an edible gel) which makes them an acceptable feed grade ingredient. Hydrolyzed feathers have been assigned the (IFN) International Feed Number 5-03-795 and can appear on a label as "Poultry By-products." On page 158 in the AAFCO book, Official Publication, 1994, Association of American Feed Control Officials Incorporated, they show: Hydrolyzed Poultry By-Products Aggregate is the product resulting from heat treatment, or a combination thereof, of all by-products of slaughter poultry, clean and undecomposed, including such parts as heads, feet, underdeveloped eggs, intestines, feathers and blood." The IFN assigned to this mix is 5-14-508.

Today's regulations allow the entire mix or any part of it to appear on a label as "Poultry By-products." A "Fish By-product" can contain heads, tails, intestines and blood. This fish process residue has been assigned the IFN 5-07-977. A "Meat By-product" could be viscera and blood soaked sawdust from the floors of a packing house where meat is being processed. The meat being processed can be lamb, beef, horse, or any other source. Each one has its own IFN. Some of the animal feed IFN's that contain wood shavings from the floor of a processing facility include "Dried Ruminant Waste" #1-07-526, and "Undried Processed Animal Waste Products" #5-02-790. It is important to note that the amount of wood shavings in either of these two "Meat By-products" is limited and should not be more than 35% in one and 40% in the other. When a pet food label's list of ingredients shows the word By-product you can be assured that there is NO measurable amount of meat in the ingredient. If the ingredient contained enough meat that it could be measured the pet food company would proudly list the MEAT, not just the By-product of that meat's production.

Mill Run:

An ingredient consisting of residue left after the primary food product has been extracted during a milling process. A "Corn Mill Run" would be a pulverized blend of the corn husk and cobs which are left after a milling process has removed the kernels. Mill Run is the vegetable or produce equivalent of meat's By-product.

Digest:

An animal feed-grade ingredient that must be made soluble with the use of heat and moisture. Since these ingredients are not soluble in their natural state they require this manufacturing process before they can be put into pet food. An example of this would be the feet of poultry IFN 5-07-947. When a pet food label shows "Poultry Digest" as an ingredient this could be what is in the food.

Meal:

A ground or pulverized composite of animal feed-grade ingredients. A good definition of a Meal is provided by AAFCO. They define Poultry By-product Meal: "Poultry By-product Meal consists of the ground, rendered, clean parts of the carcass of slaughtered poultry, such as necks, feet, undeveloped eggs, and intestines, exclusive of feathers, except in such amounts as might occur unavoidably in good processing practices." The IFN for this blend is 5-03-795. The only MEAT that might be in "Poultry By-product Meal" 5-03-795 is what could be left on the necks after becoming clean rendered By-products of meat production. This is not enough that the amount of meat can even be measured and thus have an ingredient listing showing any POULTRY MEAT to be in the food. You should be aware that when a food's ingredient panel list a product with the word "Meal" that the word "Meal" is not a synonym for "Meat." The word Meal only means that the product has been ground or pulverized.

Gluten:
The sticky substance in wheat or corn starch that gives the starch its tough elastic quality. It is used to hold together the pulverized composite of animal feed-grade ingredients.

Digestibility Test:
A test to see how much time it takes a food solid to break down in a strong laboratory acid. There are companies that are claiming the food which passes this test in the shortest amount of time provides the best nutrition for all animals. But the word digestibility is not a synonym for the word nutritious. Just because a food solid can be broken down in an acid does not mean the animal eating it can nutritionally use that kind of food. Not all dogs or cats have the same nutritional acceptance of any one food source. Since pet foods are made from many different food sources we could thus be making the proverbial comparison between apples and oranges. It would be a mistake to judge any food's total nutritive value on one test demonstrating how fast it breaks down in laboratory acid. Comparing pet foods by using a Digestibility Test is valid only if the foods being tested are of equal nutritional value for the animal that will be eating them. Then the faster a food breaks down the easier it is for the animal's digestive system to make use of it.

If you are now buying a pet food with words you don't understand on the label you might try this: contact the manufacturer and ask them for their definitions. If they do not give them to you in words you, the buyer, can understand then maybe it's time to consider home cooking your pet's food. You'd know what was in the food, and for thousands of years before commercial pet food was available (just 85 years ago), that's what pet owners successfully did.

Each breed of dog has

physical or temperamental characteristics

that are different from any other breed.

The question is

NOT IF *those characteristics affect*

a breed's nutritional requirements,

BUT HOW MUCH *do they affect a*

breed's nutritional requirements?

WE SHOULD KNOW:

Because the energy levels

among the different breeds are different

their nutritional requirements for food calories

would also be different.

LIFE CYCLE CHANGES
THAT CHANGE
NUTRITIONAL REQUIREMENTS

As your dog goes through different stages of the life cycle, its nutritional needs change substantially. Here are a few guidelines to follow for: (1) puppies, (2) the maintenance years, (3) pregnant and lactating bitches, (4) older dogs and (5) nutritional changes due to stress.

(1) **Puppies**

After weaning, feed each puppy a high fat and carbohydrate diet in small dosages 3 or 4 times per day. Once the puppy has reached 40 to 50 percent of its adult weight, change feeding schedule to twice per day. Remember a pup's nutritional requirements can be *6 to 10 times* more than adult maintenance requirements. This includes requirements for most vitamins and minerals when measured on a *per-kilogram of body weight* basis. This means an active 6 pound puppy can use the same dose as a 60 pound adult dog of the same breed. There are some breeds of dogs that are still puppies (nutritionally speaking) even after they have reached their full adult size. To treat them as adults, just because they have the body size of an adult, can rob them of nutrients that their body still requires to build good bones, teeth, muscles, coats, etc. So consider your breed of dog and **nutritionally treat a puppy like a puppy** until it has reached the adult maintenance stage of life **regardless of its body size**.

(2) **The maintenance years**

When the dog has developed to the adult stage of life it should be placed on a maintenance diet that will supply its dietary requirements under normal living conditions. This period could be called the "carefree years for feeding" for the average dog owner. The feeding times can be reduced to once daily and the amount should remain constant. Problems are few but normally arise from either a change of diet or the owner killing the dog through ignorance (*but with love*) by giving it unhealthy treats such as table scraps, cookies, etc. We should remember that the maintenance years are just what the words say; they are a time to maintain a steady dietary program.

(3) Pregnant and Lactating Bitches

During the time that a bitch is pregnant and lactating I suggest that you make the following adjustments in her daily dietary program: Begin to feed her more frequently, but decrease the amount of food given at each feeding. Increase the carbohydrate content of the food by about one-third while keeping the protein content at the same level. This can be done by putting her on a combination of her regular maintenance food and the same food that you will be feeding the puppies when they arrive. Most commercial puppy food is also higher in the vitamins and minerals that can be passed on to the puppies that are developing in her womb. If you use a supplement, increase her vitamin and mineral supplementation by 50%. **Do not imbalance her system with additional calcium or any other single mineral.** The balance of minerals is very important during this time both for the mother and the puppies. Continue with these changes until the puppies are weaned. After the puppies are weaned and her milk supply dries up, return the bitch to her standard maintenance dietary program.

(4) Older Dogs

Just as some breeds develop slower and need to be kept on a puppy formula longer, there are some breeds that reach the geriatric stage of life at later or earlier times than the *average breed*. When your dog reaches this stage, it becomes more difficult for it to convert protein to energy and they are normally not as active. Therefore, the protein amount in its daily food intake should be lower and the proportions of carbohydrates should be higher. Dogs reaching the geriatric stage also should be returned to the puppy feeding schedule. By changing their food to a high carbohydrate low protein blend, by increasing their feeding schedule to more than once daily, and by giving them smaller quantities of food at each feeding, you can prolong their life and make it more enjoyable.

(5) Nutritional changes due to stress and other factors

Often we create stress situations for our dogs without realizing it. At these times of stress the nutritional requirements can change dramatically in many ways. Two of these changes would be burning calories at a different rate and losing excessive amounts of body waters. Therefore, we must be aware of the types of situations that can cause stress in our dogs and be prepared to help them nutritionally through these times. An obvious stress situation would include the time of gestation and lactation for a bitch, with the birthing adding still more stress on her for that special time. However, other times of stress can be caused by a visit to the vet, entering a dog show, schooling, hunting or even vacation travel.

Not all times of relaxation for the dogs owner are times of relaxation for our pets. Dogs can experience stress any time their normal routine is changed. Also, like humans, different individuals will handle the stress differently. During these times of stress there are a few simple nutritional rules to follow. First be sure they have access to a good supply of water and do not over feed them with high protein foods. Remember that it is more work for their system to convert protein into energy than it is to convert carbohydrates. Therefore you should increase the carbohydrate % in the daily food intake. This can be done by giving them treats such as baked potatoes, pancakes, or rice cakes, during the hunt or on the way to the show, etc. Remember different breeds can assimilate carbohydrates from different sources at different rates. Therefore, you need to give the source of carbohydrate that is best for the dog you are feeding.

Here I also caution you about supplementation. If you are going to replace the B vitamins (known as "the stress vitamins") during this time, be sure you follow the six steps listed in the chapter on supplementation. Also remember that the association between the B vitamins and the other nutrients is critical. Therefore, you should deal with the stress vitamins as a part of a nutritional team and not create nutritional stress by supplementing the B vitamins alone.

Each breed of dog has
physical or temperamental characteristics
that are different from any other breed.

The question is
NOT IF *those characteristics affect*
a breed's nutritional requirements,
BUT HOW MUCH *do they affect a*
breed's nutritional requirements?

WE SHOULD KNOW:
Some ailments are genetically passed on
and are not common to all the different breeds.

&

Because the ailments have a direct effect
on the dogs nutritional requirements
those ailments make that breed's
nutritional requirements different
from all other breeds.

A HOME HEALTH CHECK
FOR SYMPTOMS OF
NUTRITIONAL PROBLEMS

You can tell whether your dog is getting good nutrition, IF you know what to look for. When you see the exterior results of good nutrition, you can be confident that the internal organs and systems are also healthy. Good nutrition helps your dog resist infections and disease so that it can live a longer, more productive life.

EYE COLOR
(membrane under lower lid)
Indicates proper assimilation of - Iron and other minerals

If poor - light or white in color
If good - darker in color (pink to red)

GUMS AND MOUTH TISSUE
(color and firmness)
*Indicates proper assimilation of - Vitamins, minerals
and amino acids*

If poor - loose on teeth, bleeding, light color, white spots
If good - firm on teeth, no bleeding when rubbed, darker color

SKIN CONDITION
Indicates proper assimilation of - Protein and fatty acids

If poor - dry, flaky, or can develop "hot spots"
If good - smooth and pliable

SKIN CONDITION
Indicates proper amounts of fluids

If poor - hangs on body, is not pliable
If good - returns to body shape when pulled away

COAT CONDITION
Indicates proper assimilation of - Protein and fatty acids

If poor - dry, brittle, dull in color
If good - soft, glossy, bright color

ENERGY LEVEL
Indicates proper assimilation of - Vitamins and Minerals

If poor - listless and tires easily
If good - more energetic
or
If poor - nervous to "hyper"
If good - calmer and less nervous

MUSCLE TONE
*Indicates proper assimilation of - Vitamins, minerals
and trace minerals*

If poor - cramping after prolonged or strenuous exercise
If good - reduced muscle cramping from strenuous exercise

A note of caution:
Please do not rely on nutritional home remedies for your dog if your dog needs the attention of a veterinarian.

A PRODUCT FORMULATED FOR THE NUTRITIONALLY AVERAGE DOG

We can calculate the statistical average weight of all dogs in the country (46.7 pounds) or the statistical average height of all the dogs in the country (16.5 inches). But is the averaged sized dog also this country's nutritionally average dog? Which single breed of dog represents the average size of all breeds?

Dogs' body weights range from 1 pound to 235 pounds, with a height range of 5 inches to 35 inches. Their coats range from long to short, smooth to coarse, single to double - in every imaginable color. Their dispositions range from the hyper active and nervous to the laid back and listless. Not all breeds suffer from all the same ailments. The list of ailments the different breeds can suffer from includes: Hot Spots, Bloat, Dysplasia, respiratory problems, Hyper Thyroid, Hypo Thyroid, Progressive Retinal Atrophy, Heart Failure, Worms, Cataracts, Snow Nose, Eczema, Dwarfism, Hemophilia, Kidney Failure, Liver Failure, Torsion, Enclampsia, Cyst, Black Tongue, Slipped Stifle, Temperature Sensitive, Monorchidism, Dermoid Sinus, tumors, Collie Eye, Von Willebrand's Disease, etc.

Since there are so many differences among the many breeds, which one breed accurately represents the average of all the other breeds? Could we claim that the nutritionally average breed is: (1) A Labrador Retriever, which is only one of the few breeds known to produce skin oils and not skin dander like most other breeds? (2) A Collie that needs ten times the amount of vitamin D than other breeds? (3) A Beagle that has a different requirement for vitamin A than other breeds? When commercial manufacturers of all-breed dog foods test their products, which breed should they use? Obviously, whatever breed they use, that breed is not going to be the nutritionally average breed of dog. It will not be a good representative for all the other breeds. **The nutritionally average breed of dog does not exist!**

Testing a dog food formula on one breed, cannot develop a product that will meet the nutritional needs for all the different breeds. Developing all-breed dog foods by selective testing with only one breed would be the same as developing an all-breed dog grooming product after doing research on only a hairless breed. Even after testing the product on ten breeds that shed their coats, we should not expect the product to be correct for breeds that do not shed.

The different breeds of dogs *all* have genetic differences. *One genetic difference is: they all have different nutritional requirements.* The nutritional requirements of the many breeds are so varied that no one single all-breed dog food can satisfy all their needs, or can even be considered safe for all the different breeds. I calculate the odds of an all-breed dog food being NUTRITIONALLY CORRECT for any single breed of dog at less than one-one thousandths of one percent.

In the United States there are many all breed dog food companies collectively producing hundreds of different dog food formulas at any one time. Each of these companies is telling us that the formula they have is good for our breed of dog. Then they keep changing their formulas, looking for the ideal all-breed food. They can stop looking for this ideal all-breed food blend since it will never be found. They might as well take the next one hundred thousand years and devote their research laboratories to developing a nutritionally average dog.

All-breed dog foods cannot provide what all the different dogs need. However, they do provide dog owners with what they want. As dog owners we want to be able to go to the store and get a prepackaged food that is easy to put into the dog's dish and won't take up much room in the garage. We want a product that will produce a small firm stool and is easy to clean up. We want it to be CONVENIENT. Because this is what we want, this is what commercial all breed dog food companies give us.

The commercial dog food companies can give us both what we want and also what our dogs need TODAY! To do this, all they have to do is focus on a specific segment of the market instead of trying to cover it all with a single product. Ideally it would be best if they provided us with breed specific dog foods. It is my hope, that in the future, some large dog food company will come through and do the job right by providing foods formulated to the needs of the dogs eating them.

For the commercial dog food companies to provide both what we want and what our dogs need, we must be willing to pay the price. Both manufacturing and marketing costs would increase. We also would need to be willing to give up some of the convenience present marketing methods provide. *We know that dog food should be breed specific. Until we are willing to pay the higher price for what we know to be correct, our dogs will continue to pay **the price of their life** for our convenience.*

THE HOME COOKING
ALTERNATIVE

In Grandma's day, just eighty-five years ago, there were no commercial dog foods for her to buy. Having no choice she had to cook for her pets. Today we can buy a can or bag of dog food or do it the way Grandma had to. Home cooking will always be harder than throwing a bag of pet food into a cart, yet a growing number of people today take time to cook for pets; justifying it by claiming it's out of love, a desire to provide a healthier diet, or to save money. They have found that cooking for a single pet or a full kennel can take less than two hours per week. The equipment needed is found in the average kitchen and a beginning level cook has the skill.

Home-cooked dog food can be prepared free of harmful additives. The preservatives BHA and BHT can cause epilepsy in dogs (Washington State University studies). Ethoxyquin produces kidney and liver disorders (Hazelton Laboratories study). The government's National Research Council shows that even the antioxidant vitamin C, used as a preservative in many commercial dog foods, can cause kidney and liver problems in dogs. As I have said elsewhere, vitamin C may be a good preservative to use in human food but harmful for most dogs. The Morris Animal Foundation claims that kidney and liver disorders now rank as the second and sixth highest causes of household pet death in the U.S. Additives are found in dog foods to keep them looking good or to preserve them so they won't turn rancid while sitting in a warehouse or at the retailers. Few pet owners would argue with the fact that a pet's diet would be healthier if it was made without any additives.

Cooking a dog's food can even be cost efficient. For an eye opening cost comparison let's use figures supplied by the dog food industry. In 1995 they claimed the average dog in this country weighed 46 pounds and would consume $248.00 of commercial dog food that year. Choosing a common commercial product (one sold in most grocery stores), reading that food's ingredient listing, and following the food's feeding instructions, we see that average 46 pound dog could be fed 31/2 cups per day of a food containing the following ingredients: chicken, wheat, corn gluten meal, poultry by-products (which may be hydrolyzed feathers, or feet and heads), beef tallow, rice, dried whey, vitamins, minerals, BHA and Ethoxyquin.

To cook for the same "average dog," its owner would place the following into a large pan:

- two pounds chopped chicken meat - 79¢/lb,
- one package frozen corn (ground into a fine pulp) - 59¢,
- one pound beef tallow (or 1/2 cup of cooking oil) - 74¢/lb.

Mix, bake for one hour at 350°, cool, and break into small pieces.

To the juices add:

- fourteen finely chopped slices whole wheat bread - 25¢,
- 4 cups cooked rice - 35¢,
- 1/8th pound of shredded cheese - 65¢.

Mix all ingredients together, divide into seven reusable containers, and add: • seven pet formula multi-vitamin/mineral tablets (one in each container) - 48¢. Refrigerate.

These seven ready-to-serve home cooked meals for the "average" 46 pound dog are made with the same ingredients as those in the commercial food, except for the hydrolyzed feathers and preservatives. The home-cooked food will cost $4.64 for a one week supply. This is less than the cost of a commercial food (divide their $248.00 by 52 weeks). Preparing home-cooked meals, because we care about our pet's health, can also save us money.

Home-cooking allows us to prepare foods to meet a specific dog's nutritional needs. We know that commercial foods sold for all dogs cannot possibly meet the needs of each individual member of the canine family. Two dogs of the same breed can even have different nutritional requirements. A dog's temperament will affect its nutritional requirements. Two dogs of the same breed may look alike, yet one be active and one a permanent rug decoration. The two will have different nutritional requirements. Preparing separate recipes for these two dogs based on their individual nutritional needs would be better for the health of each one.

Dog owners today have a choice that was not even available just 85 years ago. Today you can choose to provide preservative-free diets customized to each dog's individual needs, or the preservative-filled blends of an "any-dog" formula. You can serve healthy home-cooking or feed a repetitive diet of commercial fast-foods meals.

PLEASE REMEMBER:

Do not use my one recipe for all dogs. Just as a commercial food should not be sold for all breeds, the recipe I show in this chapter should not be fed to all breeds.

You should take into consideration where the breed you are feeding originated and limit the recipe ingredients to those found in that breed's native environment. i.e., Since there are NO rice paddies in the Nordic Tundra, dogs from that environment should not be fed rice. I have listed the nutrient sources I recommend for each breed in the Breed by Breed section of this book.

If you try to develop a recipe for your dog, based on the recipe in this chapter, you should substitute the correct food sources and adjust the portions according to the weight of the breed you are dealing with. You should also adjust your recipe according to any protein / carbohydrate / fiber directions given in the Breed by Breed section.

Each breed of dog has
physical or temperamental characteristics
that are different from any other breed.

The question is
NOT IF *those characteristics affect*
each breed's nutritional requirements,
BUT HOW MUCH *do they affect*
EACH BREED'S *nutritional requirements?*

BREED BY BREED

INTRODUCTION

In the following Breed By Breed chapters I recommend what I feel are the best food sources for each breed of dog. Whether you are choosing from all the commercial feeds on the market or working with a recipe for home cooking your dog's food I hope these recommendations will assist you in making an intelligent selection.

For these recommendations I have taken the following factors into consideration: (1) the nutritional history of each breed, (2) the nutrients of each breed's native environment, (3) * the nutrients presently found in commercial dog foods, (4) the nutrients that are readily available at grocery stores or butcher shops, and (5) the nutrients that would be foreign to a dog's system and cause it nutritional distress.

*I recommend ingredients that can be found in different commercial dog foods rather than recommend a brand of food for your dog. I used to make recommendations for specific brands of dog food for specific breeds. However, I have stopped doing this because most dog food companies keep changing their formulas in search of that "ideal" all-breed dog food.

For example, recommending a specific brand of dog food can cause problems. I recommended a specific brand of food to the owner of a kennel of Bichon Frise. She fed her dogs the food I recommended and was happy with the results. A short time later the dog food company changed the sources of the minerals in their product. This change was noted in fine print under "ingredients", but essentially the label on the products bag continued to **look the same**. Since they only changed the source and not the amount of the minerals, the change went unnoticed by the buyer. Her dogs then developed kidney stones on the food that was *named the same* and *looked the same . . . . but was not the same* as the food I had recommended.

If you are feeding a commercial dog food I also hope that my requiring you to read the labels on these type of products will result in your developing the habit of reading the *entire* label each time you buy a dog food. This practice will improve your chances of detecting a formula change in your dog's food.

AFFENPINSCHER

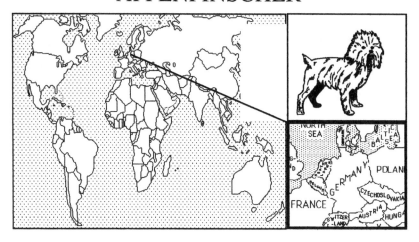

Weight Standards: m/f - 7 to 8 lbs.
Height Standards: m/f - under 10.25 inches
Coat: wiry, shaggy, in black, tan, wheaton or red
Common Ailments: slipped stifle and fractures

The Affenpinscher developed in the lowland farm area of Germany prior to the 15th century. It has a facial appearance similar to a monkey, and the literal translation of the German word "Affenpinscher" is "monkey terrier." This breed of dog is very quick afoot and at one time earned its keep as an effective stable yard ratter.

Native food supplies for this breed would have been rodents (rats, mice and other small ground animals), poultry, and farmland grains of wheat, corn and barley or alfalfa with ground vegetables of potatoes, carrots and cabbage.

For the Affenpinscher I recommend foods that are high in their carbohydrate content from potatoes and barley. The meat protein source should be a blend of horse meat and poultry. I also recommend that you avoid feeding any foods containing soy, beet pulp, white rice, fish meal or lamb to an Affenpinscher.

AFGHAN HOUND

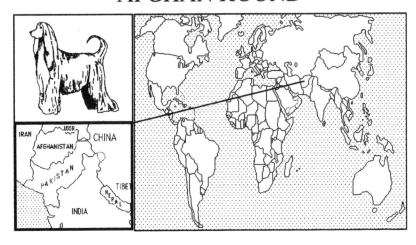

Weight Standards: m - 60 lbs., f - 50 lbs.
Height Standards: m - 27 inches, f - 25 inches
Coat: double, long top coat, soft textured, in any color
Common Ailments: cataracts, dysplasia, rashes, urinary problems

The Afghan, a sight hound, developed as a hunting dog in the Balkh, Barakzai, and Kurram valley areas of ancient Egypt, known now as Afghanistan. The earliest records of the Afghan date back some 8000 years ago to this area of ancient Egypt. These records show that they were used to hunt such animals as mountain deer, plains antelopes, hares, wolves, and snow leopards.

Native food supplies for this breed would have included the mountain deer, plains antelopes, hare, wolves, snow leopards, fox, and fowl. The Balkh, Barakzai, and Kurram valley areas also provided grain crops such as wheat, corn, barley, and brown rice. There was a form of beef cattle in this area. However, the prevalent religions forbid the use of beef as a food source for humans and dogs alike. Therefore, I feel it is unlikely that the Afghan was exposed to this form of meat.

For the Afghan hound I recommend foods with a high fiber, high carbohydrate percentage. The protein should be from sources of poultry and lamb, the carbohydrates from brown rice and wheat. For this breed I recommend you avoid foods based on soy, beet pulp, horse meat or beef and their by-products.

58

AIREDALE TERRIER

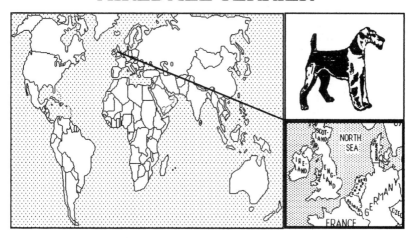

Weight Standards: m - 50 to 60 lbs., f - 45 to 55 lbs.
Height Standards: m - 23 inches, f - 22 inches
Coat: short and wiry in black or saddle with tan extremities
Common Ailments: can be hyperactive and develop skin rashes

The Airedale Terrier developed in Yorkshire County England. The human inhabitants of this area used this breed to control the otter population in order to improve the fishing. This developed a breed that, still today, is very much a water dog. An amusing Airedale trait is that they will dive under the water in pursuit of prey, a type of action that is very rare for any other breed.

A special note; The Airedale Terrier seems to develop more skin and coat problems when taken to live in arid desert climates. These problems can be corrected by feeding that Airedale a diet with higher amounts of the fatty acids.

Native food supplies found in Yorkshire County would have been meats from deer, boar, otter, and fresh water stream fish. Also vegetables of the low ground type were prevalent, such as carrots, potatoes, and cabbage.

For the Airedale I recommend foods with starch from potato and meat from beef. The food should be high in fiber content from sources such as wheat and oats. I also recommend you avoid feeding any white rice, beet pulp, or soy to the Airedale terrier.

AKITA

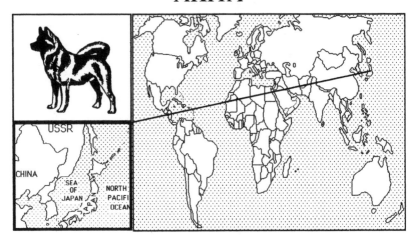

Weight Standards: m - 85 to 100 lbs., f - 75 to 85 lbs.
Height Standards: m - 26 to 28 inches, f - 24 to 26 inches
Coat: short and straight, harsh textured in any color
Common Ailments: dysplasia

The Akita developed as a hunting dog in the Japanese prefectures of Gifu, Nagano, and Toyama. At one time its ownership was restricted to the nobility, who used the breed to hunt large game such as wild boar and deer. It was also used in the blood sport of dog fighting. Today, they are used as police and guard dogs, guide dogs for the blind, and as pets.

The main meat sources in the Akita's native environment were bear, deer, wild boar, and fish. Rice was the main carbohydrate source of the area and vegetables were greens such as beans, cabbage, and tuber roots much like our sweet potato.

For the Akita, I think the best blend of protein available from commercial dog foods would contain poultry, fish, rice and wheat. For this breed I also recommend adding about 1 to 2 teaspoons of canned white Tuna daily to the commercial foods. Akita owners can also make sure their dogs receive a fat-carbohydrate-protein balance similar to the breed's native diet by using a commercial puppy formula for the breed's entire life span. Akita owners should avoid feeding any dog food containing yellow corn, beet pulp, beef or horse meats.

ALASKAN MALAMUTE

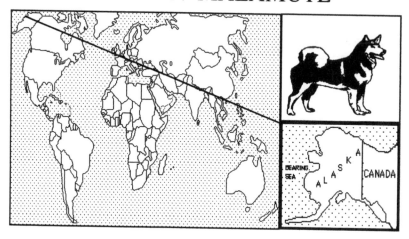

Weight Standards: m - 85 lbs., f - 75 lbs.
Height Standards: m - 25 inches, f - 23 inches
Coat: dense in texture, straight with a long top coat
Common Ailments: dwarfism, dysplasia, pigmentation

The Alaskan Malamute developed in the northern reaches of the area we now know as the state of Alaska. Named for an Inuit tribe from this area, the Alaskan Malamute tracked large game and served as a pack and sled dog. In camp it doubled as a family pet and guard dog, even serving as a nanny to the Inuit children.

This breed originated in an area where the primary food sources were whale, salmon, halibut, and seal. None of today's commercial all-breed dog foods contain those sources prevalent in the original diet of the Alaskan Malamute.

However, there are commercial foods that closely match the amino acid profile of the Alaskan Malamute's natural diet. These foods would have a combination of poultry, fish, lamb and rice in its protein base. These food sources are also high in minerals and natural occurring oils and thus would be the ideal base diet for this breed. The worst food blend for the Alaskan Malamute would contain a base of soy, beef or beef by-products, beet pulp and yellow corn.

AMERICAN COCKER SPANIEL

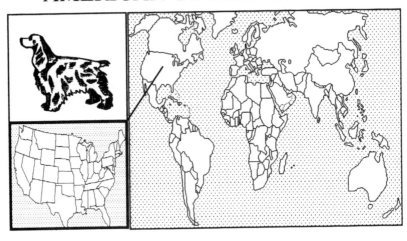

Weight Standards: m - 27 lbs., f - 25 lbs.
Height Standards: m - 15 inches, f - 14 inches
Coat: soft, long and wavy topcoat. thick undercoat,
in solid colors or parti-colored
Common Ailments: PRA, hemophilia, slipped stifle,
digestive disorders, cataracts, and ear problems

The American Cocker Spaniel originated in America from selective English Cocker Spaniel breeding stock. In America the American Cocker Spaniel is often called by the nicknames "Cocker Spaniel" or "Cocker" while the English Cocker Spaniel is referred to by its full registered name. In England the reverse is true.

This Cocker Spaniel retains many of the same nutritional requirements as the English Cocker Spaniel. However, the American Cocker Spaniel does not need a high carbohydrate diet like the English Cocker Spaniel, which remains exposed to a diet containing large quantities of carbohydrates from sources such as the potato. Yet the American Cocker must have a higher amount of the amino acid Lysine in its food than the English Cocker Spaniel.

For the American Cocker Spaniel I recommend a food blend of corn, wheat, poultry, and dairy products. Also a blend of food sources containing low carbohydrates and an average fat content. Conversely, I feel the worst blend for this breed of Cocker Spaniel would contain fish, white rice, horse meat, or soy.

AMERICAN ESKIMO

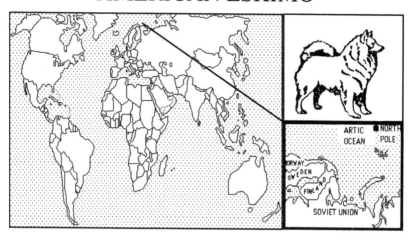

Height Standards: two classes: Miniature; m - 12 to 15 inches,
f - 11 to 14 inches, Standard; 15 to 19 inches, f - 14 to 18 inches
Coat: solid white, double, with very thick under coat and top coat
Common Ailments: hot spots, coat pigmentation problems

The American Eskimo did not develop in America at all. It can trace
its history back over 6000 years to its origins as a member of the *Nordic
Spitz* family of dog.

A heavy year around shedder this breed requires a finely balanced diet
to grow and maintain the thick and outstanding coat that is this breed's
trademark. Also the amount of coat that this breed has is equal to many
breeds of dog with a total weight of two to three times the American
Eskimo's total weight. Therefore, when considering the nutritional
requirements of this breed, one can readily see that nutrients related to
the production of coat hair are going to be in high demand.

Native food supplies for this breed would have been those found in the
Nordic Tundra. These would have included fish, seal, caribou, reindeer,
and vegetables that could grow in this environment's short growing
season.

For the American Eskimo I recommend foods that contain a blend of
fish, poultry, horse meat, wheat, and potato. I feel you should avoid
feeding a food containing white or brown rice, avocado, citrus, soy, or
lamb to this breed of dog.

AMERICAN FOXHOUND

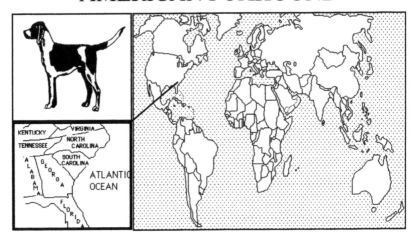

Weight Standards: m - 65 to 75 lbs., f - 60 - 70 lbs.
Height Standards: m - 22 to 25 inches, f - 21 to 24 inches
Coat: short, single, hard, black with brown and tan or tan and white
Common Ailments: a very hardy breed

The American Foxhound developed in the Southeastern area of the U. S. A. It has not always been used as a scent hound to hunt the fox. There are diary accounts claiming this breed was used to hunt Indians rather than fox or hare. These accounts were written by DeSoto's retainers when this Spanish explorer was in the Carolinas during the early 1500's. This is a breed with a well documented history. For example, we can trace a single family of this hound back three hundred years to the specific date of 1650.

Native meat supplies for this breed would have been the small game animals found in the Carolina countryside, such as the fox, raccoon, and squirrel. The crops of this area consisted of corn, wheat, beets, beans (soy), and rice.

For the American Foxhound I recommend foods that contain a blend of beef, soy, wheat, rice and corn. However, the foods you should avoid feeding an American Foxhound are those containing fish meal, poultry or lamb.

AMERICAN PIT BULL TERRIER (UKC)
AMERICAN STAFFORDSHIRE TERRIER (AKC)

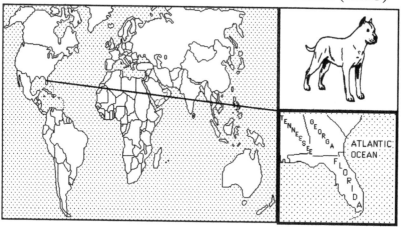

Weight Standards: m - 55 to 70 lbs., f - 40 to 55 lbs.
Height Standards: m - 18 to 19 inches, f - 17 to 18 inches
Coat: short, smooth, single in a variety of colors
Common Ailments: dysplasia, heart & respiratory problems, bloat

The American Pit Bull Terrier / American Staffordshire Terrier developed in the area now known as Florida, U.S.A. Selected stock of the Staffordshire Bull Terrier were imported from England for their development. This breed has been known by a series of names: AMERICAN PIT BULL TERRIER (UKC-1898), Yankee Terrier, Pit Bull Terrier, Half and Half, and American Bull Terrier. The American Kennel Club first accepted this breed in 1935 as the AMERICAN STAFFORDSHIRE TERRIER. This breed has been used for dog fighting and, if trained for that purpose, is very good at it. However, if it is not trained to be a warrior, it can make a good house pet, is very good with children, and is a warm and loving companion.

Native food supplies for this breed would have been the crops and meats of colonial Florida. These included yellow corn, soy meal, rice, venison, and fish.

For this breed I recommend foods that contain soy, corn, brown rice, beef, and poultry. Since this breed needs a high fiber - low carbohydrate diet, you should avoid feeding a food with a high fat or a starch content from potato.

AMERICAN WATER SPANIEL

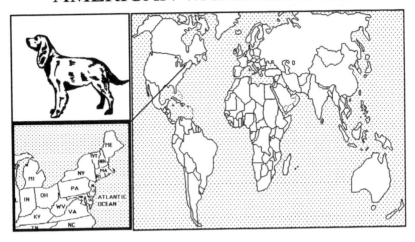

Weight Standards: m - 28 to 45 lbs., f - 25 to 45 lbs.
Height Standards: m/f - 15 to 18 inches
Coat: short, curly, chocolate
Common Ailments: hot spots (hair loss and dry coat)

It is believed **the American Water Spaniel** developed in the Northeastern part of the U.S.A. However, this cannot be confirmed and many of the first written reports about this breed came from sportsmen in the Midwestern states. It is a very good water retriever and uses a unique swimming motion like a seal. It is one of the few breeds that does not produce skin dander. This makes it ideal for people who have allergies to dogs' skin dander. This breed is one of the few breeds known to produce a skin oil. This gives the breed a requirement for higher amounts of the fatty acids than most other breeds.

Native food supplies for this breed would have been those found from the Midwestern to Northeastern U.S. These included yellow corn, wheat, water fowl, and fresh water fish.

For the American Water Spaniel, I recommend foods containing a blend of poultry, lamb, fish meal, wheat, and corn. I also recommend you avoid feeding this breed a food that contains white rice, soy, beet pulp, or horse meat.

ANATOLIAN SHEPHERD

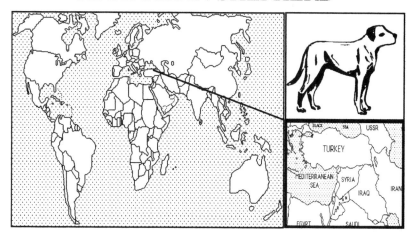

Weight Standards: m - average 100 lbs., f - average 80 lbs.
Height Standards: m - over 29 inches, f - under 27 inches
Coat: short and smooth, in buff, white, black or even tricolor
Common Ailments: hot spots and body rashes

The Anatolian Shepherd developed in the mountains of Turkey. It is a fiercely loyal guard dog and is still used to protect the flocks in its native land. Its size can be intimidating and yet it is known to be warm and loving to children.

It is known to blow its coat annually and its nutritional requirements can change during this time. For example, their requirement for protein and fat increases while the lost coat is being replaced.

Food supplies found in this breed's native area of Turkey would have included lamb, poultry, and brown rice. Any oils would have been from sources like olives or avocados.

For the Anatolian Shepherd I recommend foods made with lamb, brown rice, and poultry. The food should be high in the fatty acids from vegetable sources such as the avocado. I also feel you should avoid feeding this breed a food that contains beef, horse meat, white rice, potato, soy or beet pulp.

AUSTRALIAN CATTLE DOG

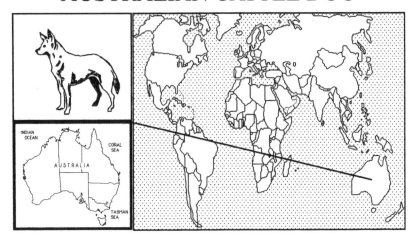

Weight Standards: m/f - 40 to 45 lbs.
Height Standards: m/f - 18 to 19 inches
Coat: dense in texture, black with tan and white speckle
Common Ailments: dysplasia, hot spots and skin rashes

The Australian Cattle Dog developed in Australia in the early 1800's. This breed can trace its heritage back to being a direct descendant of four specific breeds: the Dingo, the Blue Merle Highland Collie, the Dalmatian and the Black and Tan Kelpie. It originally herded cattle in the rough outback of Australia. Here it developed not only its nutritional requirements but its legendary stamina and endurance.

Native food supplies for this breed would have been those found in the Australian outback (a high desert environment) and would have included ground vegetables, wheat, oats and meats from beef, rabbit, and kangaroo. A special note concerning the meats; all the meats from this area have a very low fat to muscle ratio.

For the Australian Cattle dog I recommend low fat / high fiber foods with a blend of beef, corn, and wheat. I also recommend that you avoid feeding an Australian Cattle dog any soy, white rice, beet pulp, poultry or fish.

AUSTRALIAN TERRIER

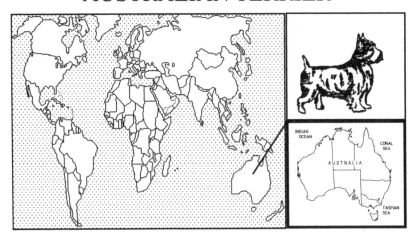

Weight Standards: m/f - 12 lbs. to 14 lbs.
Height Standards: m/f - average 10 inches
Coat: harsh textured & straight, colors of blue & tan or sandy red
Common Ailments: very hardy with few ailments reported

The Australian Terrier developed in the mountain foothills of Australia as both a ratter and a watchdog at the mines. The Australian Terrier performs both of these functions well. It is a relatively new breed of dog that was created by crossbreeding several different terrier breeds. One distinguishing feature of the Australian Terrier is its topknot, which may indicate it has relatives in common with the Dandie Dinmont Terrier. This is a very easy breed to keep in a small apartment or a confined area.

Native food supplies for this breed would have been rodents, poultry, and mutton with grains of wheat or barley found in Australian foothills.

For the Australian Terrier I recommend foods that contain horse meat, poultry, lamb, and wheat. However, I feel you should avoid feeding this Terrier any high carbohydrate foods or food containing soy or ocean fish protein.

BASENJI

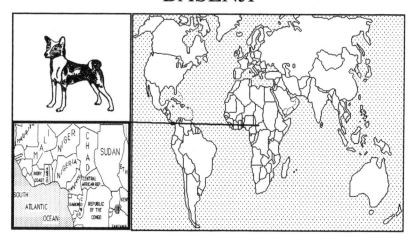

Weight Standards: m - 25 lbs., f - 23 lbs.
Height Standards: m - 17 inches, f - 16 inches
Coat: short, silky smooth, single in tan, black or red with white
Common Ailments: congenital hemollytic anemia, hyperactive

The Basenji developed in Central Africa as a sight hunter. It is not a mute dog, yet it is known as the "barkless dog." The sound that the Basenji makes is somewhere between a chortle and a yodel. In their native Africa they hunt small game by pointing, holding, and then upon command, driving the game into a net after the hunter is in position. They are also used as retrievers for the game that takes flight.

Native food supplies for this breed would have been the African desert partridge and rabbit combined with a local form of the grains wheat and rice. Another staple of their diet would have been a tuber root that is very similar to the peanut.

For the Basenji I recommend foods that contain their protein from beef and horse meats blended with poultry. The carbohydrate sources should be from brown rice and wheat. You should avoid feeding a Basenji any foods containing soy, beet pulp, fish, lamb or white rice.

BASSET HOUND

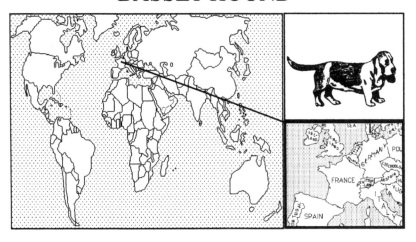

Weight Standards: m/f - average 50 lbs.
Height Standards: m/f - under 15 inches
Coat: short and smooth in brown or red with white
Common Ailments: respiratory problems (snore) and an overeater

The Basset Hound developed in France. Basset is the French word meaning "low set" and for a breed that weighs about 50 pounds they are *very* low set. They may appear to be overweight due to a loose coat that will hang in folds on their body. However, I must point out that this breed does not normally have a body weight problem. The first Basset hounds in this country appeared after the American Revolution when Lafayette presented them as a gift of state to George Washington. The Basset has a very keen sense of smell. Their long low set ears also help cup the scent during a hunt. Their short legs can cover an amazing amount of ground in a short time and, therefore, they can hunt game such as the fleet rabbit or deer.

Native meat supplies for this breed would have been venison, rabbit, mutton, and poultry. The farm crops were wheat, corn, and beets.

For the Basset Hound I recommend foods with poultry, lamb, wheat and corn. However, you should avoid feeding a Basset Hound any soy meal, horse meat, beef or its by-products, fish or white rice.

BEAGLE

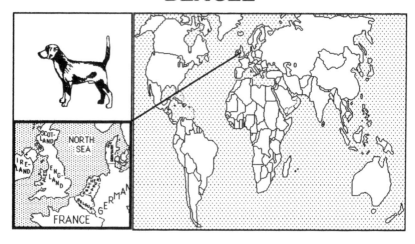

Weight Standards: two classes m/f - 13" and under -
15 to 20 lbs., 13" to 15" - 20 to 30 lbs.
Height Standards: two classes m/f - 13" and under
and over 13" but not exceeding 15"
Coat: short, smooth textured, in black with white and tan
Common Ailments: A very hardy breed with few ailments

The Beagle is a very active scent hound that originated in England. It is one of the oldest pure-bred breeds known, with a written history that dates from a time before the Norman Invasion of England in 1066. The Celtic tribesmen who hunted with this breed also named it. The Beagle's name comes from the Celtic word beag meaning "small."

I note that when hunting, the Beagle requires high carbohydrate snacks. The Beagle burns calories at an exceptional rate during times of stress or work. Like other breeds, they are unable to store the carbohydrate to burn for this energy and a heavy demand on their protein energy stores can cause muscle cramping. The Beagle also will require larger intakes of water during times of stress or work.

The Beagle originated in an area of England where its primary food sources would have been beets, potatoes, mutton, wheat, corn, rabbit, and poultry. Thus a blend of these foods, which are high in carbohydrates and have a high fat to protein ratio, would be the ideal base diet for the Beagle. Conversely, the worst blend would contain fish, rice, beef or beef by-products, horse meat, or soy.

BEARDED COLLIE

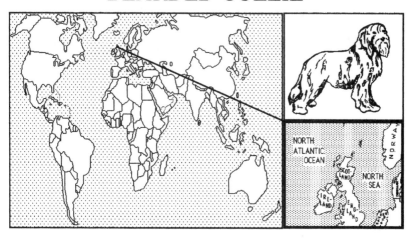

Weight Standards: m/f - average 50 lbs.
Height Standards: m/f - average 22 inches
Coat: medium length double coated with a very soft top coat
Common Ailments: dysplasia, skin rashes, hot spots
and other skin and coat problems

The Bearded Collie developed in the southern mainland of Scotland in the 1700's. For centuries it has worked as the Scottish Highlanders' able assistant, both as a drover and as a sheepdog.

A special note: Breeders have confirmed that this breed's requirement for minerals, which it can assimilate, is very different from the rough or smooth coated Collies. ie. The wrong source of the mineral calcium can cause kidney stones. Therefore, I recommend that any dietary calcium for this breed be from bone meal, and that you avoid dolomite or oyster shell forms.

Native food supplies for this breed would have been those found in the southern mainland of Scotland. These included mutton, goat, poultry, and low ground vegetable crops of potatoes, cabbage, and carrots.

For the Bearded Collie, I recommend foods low in fat that have a blend of poultry, lamb, wheat, and potato. However, you should avoid feeding a blend of soy, fish yellow corn, and horse meat or its by-products to a Bearded Collie.

BEDLINGTON TERRIER

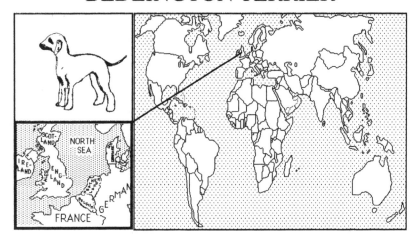

Weight Standards: m/f - 17 to 23 lbs.
Height Standards: m - 16.5 inches, f - 15.5 inches
Coat: coarse, short and curly, needs to be stripped
Common Ailments: PRA and other eye problems, liver
and kidney disorders, hyper thyroid

The Bedlington Terrier developed in the area of Rothbury, England. It hunted otter, coursed rabbit, and worked as a pit fighter. In the NRC *Nutrient Requirements of Dogs* , the Bedlington Terrier was one breed used in the testing of copper requirements. Copper is needed to form red blood cells in all dogs. These tests showed that this breed has copper requirements that are totally unique and very low. Yet, I stress the importance of providing copper to the Bedlington. I also stress that the Bedlington's copper be balanced to other nutritional team members as outlined in the chapter "Nutritional Teams." For this breed, the copper should not be from a sulfate source.

Native food supplies for this breed would have been otter, fresh water fish, rodents, oats, and wheat, - such as those found in the area of Rothbury, England.

For the Bedlington I recommend foods that are a blend of horse meat and fish with wheat and oats. I also recommend that you avoid feeding a food with soy, lamb, white rice or yellow corn to this breed.

BELGIAN MALINOIS

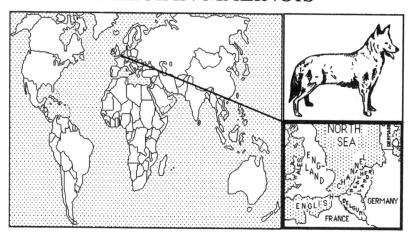

Weight Standards: m - 65 to 75 lbs., f - 55 to 65 lbs.
Height Standards: m - 24 to 26 inches, f - 22 to 24 inches
Coat: short and straight in light tricolors
Common Ailments: the hardiest of the Belgian herding breeds

The Belgian Malinois developed near the city of Malines, Belgium, which is a northern city close to the border of the Netherlands and North Sea. Often this breed is called the short coated Belgian Tervuren. Yet these two breeds are very different. The Belgian Malinois has a requirement for less fiber in its diet than the other Belgium herding breeds. Its requirement for minerals is also unique. The Malinois can best use mineral sources associated with a coastal environment rather than those found in the environment of Laeken, which would be the native environment of the Tervuren.

Native food supplies for the Belgium Malinois breed would have been associated with the sea foods of the North Sea. The Maline's area also provided goat, poultry, cabbage, and wheat.

For the Belgian Malinois I recommend foods that are low in fiber and have protein from poultry, ocean fish, and wheat. You should avoid feeding the Mal any soy, beet pulp (good for the Tervuren), horse meat or beef.

BELGIAN SHEEPDOG

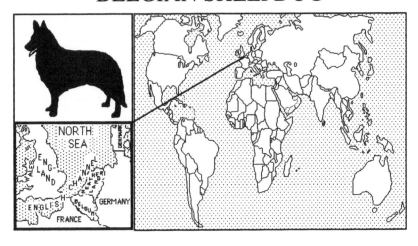

Weight Standards: m - 65 to 75 lbs., f - 55 to 65 lbs.
Height Standards: m - 24 to 26 inches, f - 22 to 24 inches
Coat: solid black, straight and long
with an undercoat that gives it a dense appearance
Common Ailments: liver and kidney disorders

The Belgian Sheepdog developed in the city of Groenendael, Belgium. This city is on the border of Luxembourg and is nestled in the foothills of that country's Alpine Mountains. In most of the world this breed is called the "Groenendael" and it is only in America that it is called the "Belgian Sheepdog." They are very intelligent and have been used throughout Europe for police work. They make great pets since they are very faithful companions and loyal watchdogs.

When properly fed, this breed's solid black coat is beautiful. However, when fed protein with a low amount of the amino acid Phenyalanine, its coat can lose its pigmentation and that beautiful black color can turn to a dull orange.

Native food supplies for this breed would have included beets, (which are the main vegetable crop of the area), wheat, mutton, poultry, and a limited amount of beef.

For the Belgian Sheepdog I recommend foods from low fat poultry and high carbohydrate beet, blended with wheat and beef. You should avoid feeding a commercial food with soy, fish, yellow corn or horse meat to this breed.

BELGIAN TERVUREN

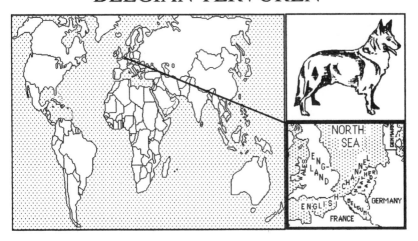

Weight Standards: m - 65 to 75 lbs., f - 55 to 65 lbs.
Height Standards: m - 24 to 26 inches, f 22 to 24 inches
Coat: long, dense and straight in tricolor
Common Ailments: hot spots and skin rashes

The Belgian Tervuren developed in the Laeken area of Belgium. The Laeken area of Belgium is on the border of Germany. It would have provided a very different environment than the foothills of the Alps or the coastal region next to the North Sea where the other two AKC recognized Belgian herding breeds developed. This breed is a very special working dog that earned a place in history during World War I as a messenger carrier. One major casualty of the war could have been the extinction of this breed of dog. Many of them were lost while performing their duty in battle. However, thankfully, after the war European dog fanciers worked to save this breed from extinction.

Their native environment would have supplied foods including beef, oats, beets, cabbage, and other leafy greens. Note: the meats from this environment all contained a high amount of body fat to muscle ratio.

For the Belgian Tervuren I recommend foods from beef, wheat, beet pulp, and oats. These foods should be high in their animal fat content. Avoid any food that contains soy, fish, corn, white rice or horse meat for this breed.

BERNESE MOUNTAIN DOG

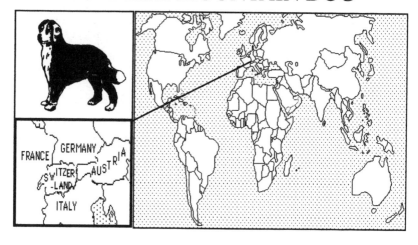

Weight Standards: m - 80 to 105 lbs., f - 75 to 90 lbs.
Height Standards: m - 23 to 27.5 inches, f - 21 to 26 inches
Coat: medium long, flat, soft, wavy topcoat, black with rust & white
Common Ailments: bloat, dysplasia, hot spots

The Bernese Mountain Dog developed in the Bern Region of the Swiss Alps. They herded livestock and worked as cart dogs to transport goods and produce to market. Due to the high mineral content in the soil and water supplies of the Bern Region of Switzerland, this breed developed a need for a unique balance of minerals such as selenium, iron, zinc and manganese in its diet.

The alpine mountain environment around Bern remained very cold year round and therefore produced a dog with more body fat than breeds that developed in warmer climates. Most animals that could survive the Bern Valley's alpine environment also had this extra body fat. Since these were the animals that formed the meat base of the Bernese Mountain Dog's noncommercial diet, today's Bernese Mountain Dog also will do best on food sources with high fat content. Native foods that would have been in this breed's diet would have included goats, sheep, pigs, chicken, and low ground vegetables.

I recommend food blends that contain a blend of poultry, lamb, and wheat as the best for this breed. Avoid foods that contain yellow corn, soy, ocean fish, beef or horse meat and their by-products.

BICHON FRISE

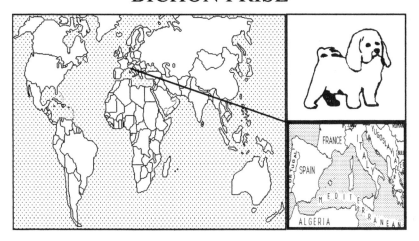

Weight Standards: m/f - 11 to 15 lbs.
Height Standards: m/f - 8 to 12 inches
Coat: thick, short, double, white
Common Ailments: skin and ear problems

The Bichon Frise's home port was in the Mediterranean area of what is now France and Italy. They became popular world wide by accompanying the sailors from their home ports around the world and were used as a trade item. The name Bichon Frise when translated from French means curly-coated lapdog, a name that this breed definitely earned. The Bichon is one of the few breeds that can assimilate the minerals that are from sulfate sources. I credit this unique feature to the soil from their native environment being primarily limestone with mineral deposits having molecular forms similar to commercial sulfate sources. This is important since the Bichon, like most other breeds of dog, will develop kidney stones when the dietary minerals are from sources they cannot assimilate.

The primary food sources of this breed's native environment included fish, goat, wheat, green vegetables, and carbohydrates of the type found in pasta.

For this breed of dog I recommend a blend that contains poultry, lamb, fish, rice, avocado, and wheat. These should provide the closest amino acid balance to that required by the Bichon Frise. Conversely, I feel the least desirable blend would contain beef or its by-products, with soy and yellow corn meal.

BLACK AND TAN COONHOUND

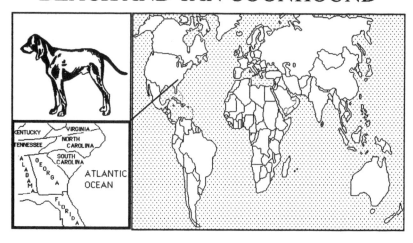

Weight Standards: m - 80 to 90 lbs., f - 65 to 75 lbs.
Height Standards: m - 26 to 28 inches, f - 23 to 26 inches
Coat: short and smooth in black and tan
Common Ailments: hypo thyroid, skin and coat problems

The Black and Tan Coonhound developed in the Southeastern U.S.A. (the Carolinas). It is a scent hound that only gives voice after he has successfully treed his quarry. The Black and Tan Coonhound is a very powerful dog that has the courage required to keep a mountain lion or bear at bay until the hunter arrives, as well as the quickness and stamina required to hunt raccoon, and deer.

Native food supplies for this breed would have been the same as for the early Carolina colonists. This area provided meats from deer, bear, wild boar, and turkey. Rice was a larger commercial crop than tobacco or cotton in the Carolinas before the Civil War and therefore would have been a staple of this breed's diet. The other native vegetable crops of soy bean and flax are the reasons this breed developed its requirement for high amounts of dietary vegetable oil.

For the Black and Tan Coonhound I recommend foods that contain lots of rice blended with beef or horse meat, corn, wheat, and beet pulp. You should avoid feeding a Black and Tan Coonhound any fish or lamb.

BLOODHOUND

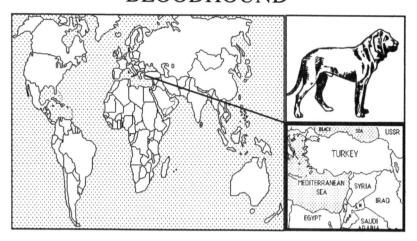

Weight Standards: m - 90 to 110 lbs., f - 80 to 100 lbs.
Height Standards: m - 25 to 27 inches, f - 23 to 25 inches
Coat: short and smooth in black or liver with tan
Common Ailments: bloat, thyroid problems

The Bloodhound developed prior to the twelfth century in the vicinity of Constantinople. This was a seaport in the country we now know as Turkey. They have been blessed with a scenting ability that is unparalleled by any other breed of dog. Bloodhounds have a genetic tendency to hypothyroidism, which is an inability of the thyroid gland to manufacture sufficient amounts of thyroxine. Within the thyroid gland iodine molecules and protein molecules join to make thyroxine. Therefore, this process can be helped by providing the proper form of iodine for their thyroid gland to use. I feel the best form of iodine for the Bloodhound is the natural form found in sea kelp, and the worst form is any one of the artificial isotopes of iodine.

Native food supplies for this breed would have been from their seaport environment and included ocean fish, pork, goat, wheat, brown rice, high carbohydrate vegetables, and fruits such as avocado, olive or fig.

For the Bloodhound I recommend food with a blend of wheat, brown rice, avocado, and poultry. However, I feel you should avoid feeding a Bloodhound any beef and its by-products, soy, beets, lamb, or white rice.

BORDER COLLIE

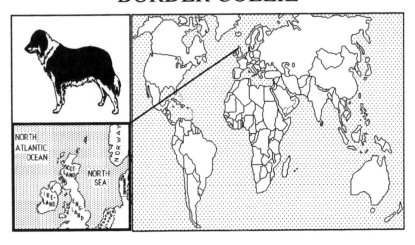

Weight Standards: m - 45 to 55 lbs.; f - 35 to 45 lbs.
Coat: ranges from short to long; black with white markings,
also tricolor, liver and white, and blue and red merle.
Common Ailments: Hot spots, collie eye, von Willebrand's disease

The Border Collie originated in Scotland and is considered by some to be the grandparent of all collies. They are bred for their intelligence and their ability to perform rather than how they conform to a set of physical standards. They are a true working dog. While performing their duties, they can cover a distance of over 100 miles without rest in a single day.

The primary food sources found in the Border Collie's native environment would have included potatoes, wheat, corn, lamb, fish, and poultry. The Border Collie requires its mineral complex to be from sources that are similar to those found in a coastal environment. Breeders have indicated that the minerals from other sources can produce many dietary problems for this breed.

I recommend a blend of foods that are high in their carbohydrate-to-protein ratio as best for a Border Collie. The food sources should be from potatoes, wheat, corn, lamb, fish, and poultry. Food sources that should be avoided by the Border Collie are soy, beet pulp, avocado, or white rice.

BORDER TERRIER

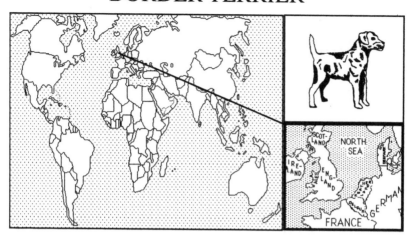

Weight Standards: m/f - average 15 lbs.
Height Standards: m - 13 to 15.5 inches, f - 11.5 to 14 inches
Coat: short and harsh, needs to be stripped,
in many colors; Wheaton, grizzle or tan being the most popular
Common Ailments: a very hardy breed with few ailments

The Border Terrier developed in the Cheviot Hills on the northern border of England. Once called the Coquetdale Terrier it has been a favorite of the farmers in its native land for centuries. The gentry desired the Border Terrier's size so that they would have a dog that could "go to ground" after a fox, yet keep up with the horses during a chase. Its most unique physical characteristic is a very distinctive head with the physical appearance like that of an otter.

Native food supplies for this breed would have been fox, hare, and rodents - with wheat and low ground vegetables (potato, carrot, and cabbage) that could be grown in the rocky soil of the Cheviot Hills area.

For the Border Terrier I recommend foods with horse meat, wheat and yellow corn. The starch and carbohydrates should come from potatoes and not rice or beets. You also should avoid feeding a Border Terrier any soy, poultry, or white fish.

BORZOI

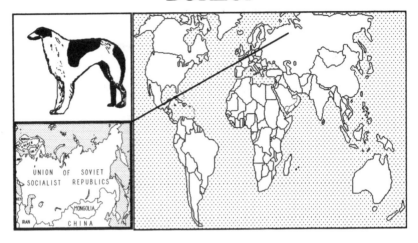

Weight Standards: m - 75 to 105 lbs., f - 60 to 90 lbs.
Height Standards: m - over 28 inches, f - over 26 inches
Coat: long, silky outer coat in white with black or tan
Common Ailments: bloat, torsion, hot spots, a picky eater

The Borzoi, once known as the *Russian Wolfhound*, developed in Russia as a hunting companion to the aristocracy. The history of this breed can be traced for centuries with a set of breed standards first established in the 1600's. The history books also show us that this breed almost became extinct in its native land. The Bolsheviks started slaughtering them due to their association with the aristocracy during the Russian Revolution of 1917. A sight hound, it hunted by running down and holding the prey until its human companion arrived. The prey it hunted ranged from the Russian wolf, which is a large ferocious beast in its own right, to deer and small game animals such as rabbit. To hunt this range of prey the Borzoi needed to be strong and courageous, yet also possess extreme speed and agility. All these traits are still retained by today's Borzoi.

Native food supplies for this breed would have been those naturally found in the coniferous forest and steppe grasslands of its native Russia. These included the wolf, deer, and other small game animals. This area also provided the high fiber grains of wheat and alfalfa.

For the Borzoi I recommend foods that blend beef and horse meat with wheat and yellow corn. However, you should avoid feeding a Borzoi white rice, soy, beet pulp, or fish (especially the white ocean varieties).

BOSTON TERRIER

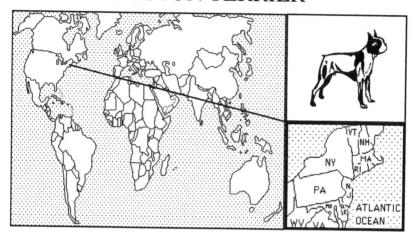

Weight Standards: m/f - around 25 lbs.
Height Standards: m/f - average 15 inches
Coat: short and smooth in black and white or brindle and white
Common Ailments: respiratory and circulatory problems,
heat and cold sensitive, eye problems

The Boston Terrier developed in the seaport city of Boston in the Northeastern United States. The American Kennel Club first registered this breed in 1893. They are descendants of a cross between a White English Terrier and the English Bulldog. Boston Terriers were originally known as Round Heads or Bull Terriers. It is a breed that keeps itself clean and is easy to maintain. It is also a breed that is very intelligent and good with children. Therefore, it is easy to see why once they were the most popular breed of dog registered in the United states.

Native food supplies for this breed would have been cattle and dairy products, wheat, beets, corn, and fish.

For the Boston Terrier I recommend foods that have beef and fish blended with beet pulp, wheat, and yellow corn. The Boston Terrier should avoid any soy products, white rice, or highly acidic foods.

BOUVIER DES FLANDRES

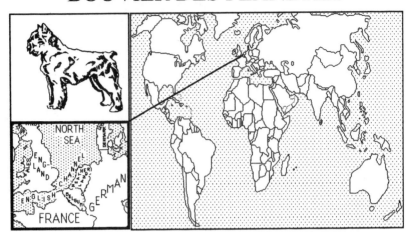

Weight Standards: m - 90 to 110 lbs., f - 80 to 95 lbs.
Height Standards: m - 23.5 to 27.5 inches, f - 22.5 to 26.5 inches
Coat: medium length, double, harsh in solid gray or black
Common Ailments: bloat, dysplasia, hot spots and skin rashes

The Bouvier des Flandres developed in the area of Brussels, Belgium. Major Police forces throughout the world use and respect this breed for their loyalty and devotion to duty. Being very intelligent, they are easy to train. However, they need an owner who will not turn over the leadership role to the dog. Their demanding personality can make life miserable for the humans in the house, if allowed to assume the role of the master. When they are allowed to assume the role of the master, they can be very hard to retrain. Their original function in life was to round up the cattle and drive them to market. Often they use these same herding skills with small children who are placed in their very capable care.

Native food supplies from the environment near Brussels, Belgium, would have included beef cattle, fish, a form of brown rice, and flax.

For the Bouvier des Flandres I recommend foods that are a blend of beef meal and fish with brown rice and wheat. This food also should have a very high vegetable oil content from wheat germ oil or linseed oil. However, I feel you should avoid feeding a Bouvier des Flandres yellow corn, soy (including soy oil coat conditioners), beet pulp, or horse meat.

BOXER

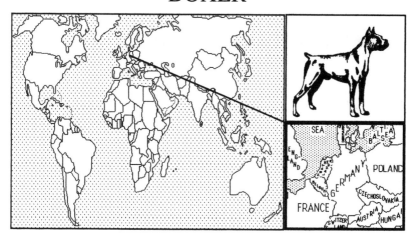

Weight Standards: m - average 70 lbs., f - around 60 lbs.
Height Standards: m - 22.5 to 25 inches, f - 21 to 23.5 inches
Coat: single, short, smooth, fawn or brindle with white
Common Ailments: bloat, tumors, digestive disorders

The Boxer originated in Germany as a medium-sized security dog. This breed was named for the manner in which it starts a fight; it makes motions with its front paws like a man when boxing.

Without the proper nutrients (high in their fiber content) the Boxer has a tendency to bloat and produce intestinal gas. This is partly due to the size and length of the boxer's colon. Other causes of gastric bloating are associated with a gland in the boxer's digestive system. This gland, the pancreas, secretes digestive enzymes such as trypsin, amylase and lypase. Tests have revealed that the Boxer's pancreas produces these digestive enzymes at a markedly different rate than those produced by the pancreas of many other breeds in the same weight category. Because of this digestive enzyme difference, an all-breed dog food may cause the Boxer to experience gastric problems not commonly found in other breeds of dogs.

The primary food sources in the Boxer's native environment were whole oat, rye, pork, and poultry. I recommend a blend of these food sources as an ideal diet because they are high in fats, fiber, and trace minerals. Conversely, the worst blend would consist of fish, soy, rice, beet pulp and horse meat or its by-products.

BRIARD

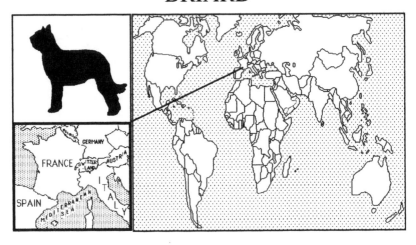

Weight Standards: m - 80 to 90 lbs., f - 70 to 80 lbs.
Height Standards: m - 23 to 27 inches, f - 22 to 25.5 inches
Coat: long and silky, slightly wavy and in any solid color but white
Common Ailments: bloat, dysplasia

The Briard developed in the area of Southern France as a herding dog for the nomadic Bask people. As the working dog of the Bask, they established themselves as excellent herding dogs, and when properly trained, they are a pleasure to watch. When they are running, their gait is so smooth that they have the appearance of floating above the ground. Marquis de Lafayette first brought them to this country in 1777 when he came from France to join Washington's staff. Some other people they have accompanied in their illustrious history have been Napoleon and Charlemagne.

Native food supplies for this breed would have been the type of vegetation grown in the middle and high latitude forests and broadleaf and broadleaf-conifer forests that the nomadic Bask traveled through in Southern France and Eastern Spain. The grains of wheat, corn, and wild rice would have been the prevalent starch and fiber sources for their dietary intake. Meat sources would have consisted of mutton and pork from the Basks' herds as well as fish from the local streams.

For the Briard I recommend foods that have a blend of lamb, fish, wheat, and brown rice. However, I suggest that you avoid feeding a Briard any soy products, beet pulp, white rice, beef, or beef by-products.

BRITTANY SPANIEL

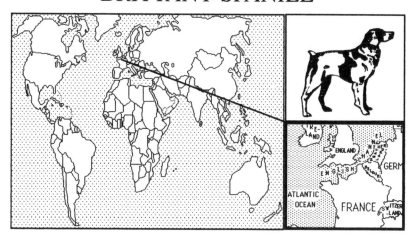

Weight Standards: m/f - 30 to 40 lbs.
Height Standards: m/f - 17.5 to 20.5 inches
Coat: short, single, wavy with feathers, liver and white
Common Ailments: very hardy with few ailments

The Brittany Spaniel developed in an area of today's France that was controlled by the kings of England during the Middle Ages. This area was a popular hunting territory for the Norman nobles whose ancestors crossed the English Channel and successfully conquered England in 1066. These Norman nobles were responsible for the development of a hunting dog, which is the same Brittany Spaniel we know today.

The primary nutrients of their native environment would have been poultry, fish of the trout family, beets, and potatoes. I note that this was a swampy area and supported few grain crops. I feel it was this factor that led to a critical difference between the Brittany Spaniel's nutritional requirements and those of the English Springer Spaniel -- especially in the area of carbohydrate needs.

Reportedly, the Brittany can utilize a higher starch and carbohydrate to protein ratio than its English cousin (The English Springer Spaniel) when the carbohydrate source is beet pulp or potatoes. The Brittany also does poorly on blends containing corn, barley or wheat, which are good for the English Springer Spaniel.

For the Brittany Spaniel, use foods with sources of poultry, lamb, and beet pulp. Avoid foods based on beef or horse meat and their by-products as well as any yellow corn, barley, wheat, or soy products.

BRUSSELS GRIFFON

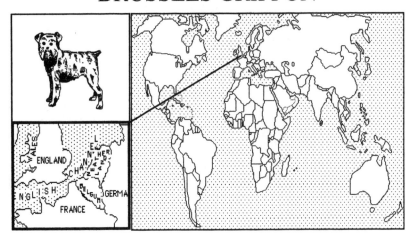

Weight Standards: m/f - 8 to 12 lbs.,
Height Standards: m/f - average 8 inches
Coat: short and thick in black tan or beige, needs stripping
Common Ailments: slipped stifle, eye and respiratory problems

The Brussels Griffon developed in the township of Brussels, Belgium, where it first earned its keep as a ratter in the stables. It then took a place beside the coachman for the hansom cabs (a horse drawn coach) from those stables. Its new duties included being the watch dog or guardian for the coach and its inhabitants.

Native food supplies for this breed would have included the stable's rodent population as well as the grains eaten by those rodents. Here, I would like to note an important nutritional requirement for the Brussels Griffon. They have a requirement for the same dietary amount of the alpha-linolenate family of fatty acids as many larger dogs from other environments. This per pound of body weight nutritional difference I attribute to their native environment's high production of the grain flax (a grain known to contain very high percentages of the alpha-linolenate fatty acids).

For this breed I recommend foods of horse meat and beef with wheat and yellow corn. The dietary fatty acids should be from grain sources similar to flax, and I recommend the forms of linseed or wheat germ oil since a Brussels Griffon can use these better than fatty acids found in animal fat or soy. Foods I suggest you avoid feeding a Brussels Griffon are soy, poultry, lamb, avocado, and white rice.

BULL TERRIER

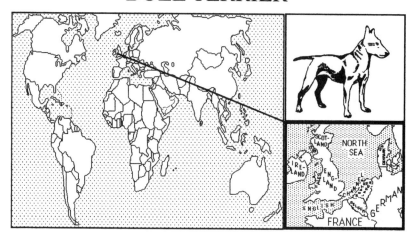

Weight Standards: m/f - 35 to 55 lbs.
Height Standards: m/f - average 18.5 inches
Coat: short and smooth in solid white or tricolored with black & tan
Common Ailments: inner ear infections, circulatory problems,
and skin rashes with hives

The Bull Terrier developed on the outskirts of London, England. They were first bred to be a pit fighter, but that soon ended. They were then taught to only defend themselves or their masters and not to seek out or provoke a fight. It was during this later stage in their history that they received their reputation of being bred by gentlemen for gentlemen. The advertising industry has exploited their clownish personality in commercials from shoes to beer. They are very fond of children and make good family pets. However, I have been told that this breed's training should start at an early age, since they tend to have a stubborn streak.

Native food supplies for this breed consisted of beef and potatoes with carrots, cabbage, and wheat. These are still the staples of the average Londoner's diet.

For the Bull Terrier I recommend foods that contain the protein from beef and wheat, the carbohydrates from potatoes, and the fiber from cabbage. However, I also recommend that you avoid feeding a Bull Terrier any white rice, avocado, soy, or ocean fish.

BULLDOG

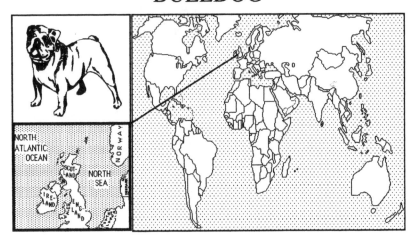

Weight Standards: m - average 50 lbs., f - average 40 lbs.
Height Standards: m - average 16 inches, f - average 14 inches
Coat: short and smooth in all colors except black
Common Ailments: heart and respiratory ailments,
skin problems, hyper thyroid, drools and snuffles

The Bulldog developed in the northern farmland counties of the British Empire where it was used in the "sport" of bull baiting. Fortunately this "sport" is gone and the Bulldog remains. It was one of the first breeds recognized by the newly organized Kennel Club of England in 1873. At this time the breed standards were established. These standards have not changed since. This breed is very strong (muscled and willed) and has taken more than one child for a walk to wherever the dog decided to go. Nutritionally the Bulldog is a breed of dog that is very slow to mature. They reach their full adult body size at about 14 months but should be nutritionally treated as a puppy until about the 30th month. This will help develop healthier bones, teeth, muscles, and coats.

Native food supplies for this breed would have been beef and dairy products blended with large quantities of high carbohydrate potatoes and cabbage. For this reason, today's Bulldog needs a food with a very high percentage of carbohydrate and fiber but not a very high amount of protein.

For the Bulldog I recommend foods high in potato type carbohydrates with the protein being from a beef, wheat, and yellow corn blend. You should avoid feeding a Bulldog any white rice, soy, poultry, or lamb.

BULLMASTIFF

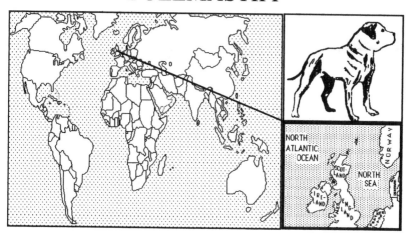

Weight Standards: m - 110 to 130 lbs., f - 100 to 120 lbs.
Height Standards: m -25 to 27 inches, f - 24 to 26 inches
Coat: short and smooth in brindle or fawn
Common Ailments: bloat, dysplasia, tumors, mouth boils

The Bullmastiff developed in Northern England where it earned its keep as a game keeper's able assistant. They patrolled the country estates of the wealthy landowners and were trained to warn the game keeper of poachers. They ran down the poacher, threw him to the ground, and held him without harm until the game keeper came. For this kind of job, they needed to be very intelligent, very territorial and very powerful. Traits originally sought in an estates Bullmastiff puppy population have now become the norm for this breed. Another norm for this breed that developed in Northern England was the Bullmastiff's unique nutritional needs.

Food supplies from the English estates played a role in the development of this breed's nutritional needs. These consisted of poultry, such as chukker or quail, meats like venison, boar or hare, and grain crops of wheat and oats.

For the Bullmastiff I recommend foods that blend equal amounts of beef with horse meat and poultry. The food also should have a very high fiber content from whole oats, wheat, and whole corn. However, I also feel that you should avoid feeding any food that contains fish or soy or any minerals that are from sulfate sources to a Bullmastiff.

CAIRN TERRIER

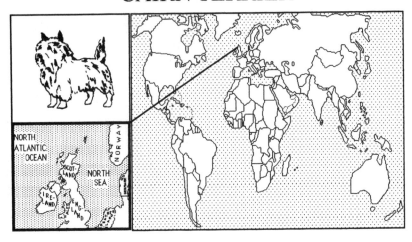

Weight Standards: m - 13 to 15 lbs., f - 12 to 14 lbs.
Height Standards: m - 10 inches, f - 9.5 inches
Coat: harsh and short and in any color except white
Common Ailments: thyroid problems

The **Cairn Terrier** developed in the Western Coastal Region of Scotland. At one time it was so popular on the island of Skye that it was called the "Short Haired Skye." However, to avoid any confusion, since there was a breed with the registered name of "Skye Terrier", the dog fanciers who first registered this breed with the English Kennel Club presented it with the name of Cairn Terrier. This terrier hunted in packs to control the fur bearing vermin, such as otter and fox that inhabited the rocky shoreline of this breed's native environment. Their name "Cairn" comes from the Galic language and means "the heap of stones where a fox would burrow."

Native food supplies for this breed would have been those that are associated with a harsh coastal North Sea environment. These included meats of the otter or fox, which inhabited the rocky cliffs, and vegetables that could grow well in the shallow rocky soil.

For the Cairn Terrier I recommend foods made of white ocean fish blended with poultry and wheat. I also recommend that you avoid feeding a Cairn any soy products, rice (both white or brown), or avocado.

CARDIGAN WELSH CORGI

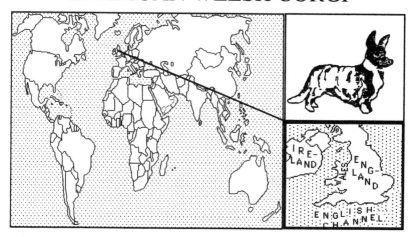

Weight Standards: m/f - average 33 lbs.
Height Standards: m/f - average 12 inches
Coat: short and harsh in tan and black with white
Common Ailments: spinal disc and digestive disorders

The Cardigan Welsh Corgi developed in the area of Cardiganshire, in the Welsh highlands over 3000 years ago. The first written report of the Cardigan comes from the Celtic tribes that inhabited the area we now know as Wales. They described a dog that was a good baby-sitter and hunter. This breed is often mistaken for the Pembroke Welsh Corgi. However, if there is a relationship between these two very different breeds, it is very distant. Opposite to the rounding up actions of the other breeds of dog that are in the AKC's herding group, the Cardigan Welsh Corgi chased the tribes' cattle. This scattered the cattle over a larger grazing area, thus insuring the herd a sufficient amount of food. This action insured survival of the cattle in a native environment that was very rocky and where grass was very scarce.

The native food supplies for all inhabitants of the Cardiganshire area, including the Cardigan Welsh Corgi, would have been the type that could survive in the rocky soil. These would have included rye, cabbage, potatoes, and carrots. Also native to this environment would have been meats of the hare, both ocean and fresh water fish, and a very stringy beef with a low fat content.

For the Cardigan Welsh Corgi I recommend foods that are a blend of fish and small amounts of beef combined with rye, oats, and yellow corn. You should avoid feeding any blend that contains white rice, soy, or beet pulp.

CHESAPEAKE BAY RETRIEVER

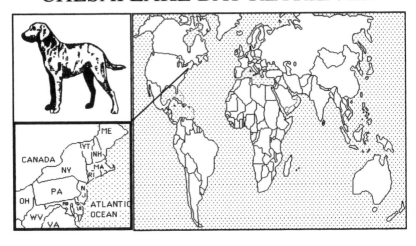

Weight Standards: m - 65 to 75 lbs., f - 55 to 65 lbs.
Height Standards: m - 23 to 26 inches, f - 21 to 24 inches
Coat: short and coarse with a thick undercoat, in brown or tan
Common Ailments: skin problems, dysplasia, liver &kidney failure

The Chesapeake Bay Retriever developed in 1807 in Maryland, U.S.A.. This is one breed that can trace its beginnings to two specific dogs named "Sailor" and "Canton." The Chesapeake is a breed that is extremely good in the home with children; yet it is known more as a hunter than a pet.

This breed has a very dense undercoat that it keeps oiled naturally when fed the proper balance of the alpha-linolenic fatty acids. This characteristic makes it a good breed for people who are allergic to the skin dander produced by most other breeds. The fact that it naturally produces these oils (only one of six breeds that does) also gives it a whole set of different nutritional requirements than those breeds that do not produce skin oil.

The native nutrients for this breeds forefathers are unknown. Yet they do well on fish and water foul, such as duck and goose (which are very high in their fat to meat ratio), and grains such as wild rice and wheat. For this breed I recommend a food blend that is high in poultry fats. Its protein should be from poultry as well. The food should contain brown, not white rice, and any other carbohydrates should be supplied by wheat. For the Chesapeake Bay Retriever it is best to avoid foods that contain beef or horse meat, lamb, beet pulp, or soy.

CHIHUAHUA

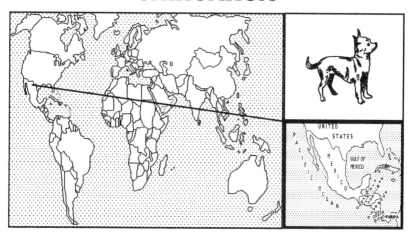

Weight Standards: m - 5 to 6 lbs., f - 4 to 5 lbs.
Height Standards: m/f - average 5 inches
Coat: two varieties; long and soft; short and soft.
Common Ailments: slipped stifle, rheumatism,
gum ailments, liver failure, and temperature sensitive

The Chihuahua that we know today was named after its area of origin, Chihuahua, Mexico. Archaeologists have given us the best account of this breed's history by finding its association with the ancient Aztecs. The Chihuahua was both a religious necessity and a working dog for the Aztec priest. It earned its keep in the temples by controlling the rodent population. Archaeologists also show that this breed lived a life span almost double to that expected by today's Chihuahua owner. I believe there is an association between this breed's unique nutritional requirements, the nutrient levels found in all-breed dog foods, and this breed's reduced life span.

Rain forests and jungles of Mexico and South America provided the native food supplies for this breed. Tropical fruits such as mango and avocado were plentiful in this environment and would have been a staple of the dietary intake. Meats were rodents or wild boar and poultry.

For today's Chihuahua I recommend foods that contain avocado blended with poultry and rice. However, I feel you should avoid feeding a food that contains beef, or beet pulp to this nutritionally delicate breed.

CHINESE CRESTED

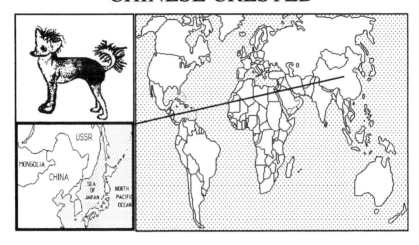

Weight Standards: m/f - 6 to 8 lbs.
Height Standards: m/f - average 5 inches
Coat: hairless except for crest on head
and fringes on feet and at tip of tail
Common Ailments: body rashes, liver failure, temperature sensitive

The Chinese Crested, a "hairless breed", developed in China as a favorite pet of the Mandarins. However, it is now extinct in that area of the world. For the last five centuries the Crested that we know today has been a resident in the West Indies and coastal port cities of South America. The Crested survived, thanks to the sailors from the Clipper Ships out of Spain and Portugal. These ships traded with China, taking this breed to other ports of call as both a food and a trade item. It is the smallest of the "hairless breeds"; such a small dog to have such a very long and colorful history.

Native food supplies for this breed would have been those from the coastal cities of China and later, South America. The primary nutrients would have consisted of ocean fish, white rice and soy products.

For the Chinese Crested Dog I recommend foods that have a blend of fish and rice. These should be low in their fiber content. I also recommend you avoid feeding this breed a food with high carbohydrate percentages or meats like beef and horse meat.

CHINESE SHAR-PEI

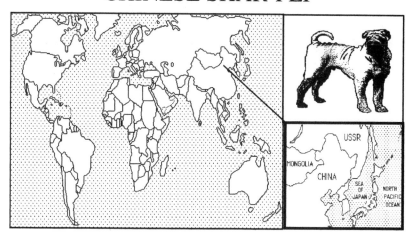

Weight Standards: m/f - 55 to 65 lbs.
Height Standards: m/f - 18 to 22 inches
Coat: Bristly textured, with loose folds, colors of solid fawn, red, black or chocolate
Common Ailments: dysplasia, bloat, eye ailments, hot spots and skin pigmentation problems

The Chinese Shar-Pei developed in China prior to the Han Dynasty (202 B.C. - 220 A.D.). This time period in China was the "*Warring States period* ". The breed of dog that emerged during this era was appropriate for the attitudes that prevailed. First bred to be fighting dogs, their owners developed a breed of dog that had very loose folds of skin so that their opponent could not easily get to a vital spot for the kill. Other physical characteristics of this breed are: they can have a blue - black tongue; the texture of their coat hair is unlike that of any other breed's; They posses a jaw structure that is totally unique in canines. These unique physical characteristics suggest that this breed is unlike any other, just like their unique nutritional requirements.

Native food supplies included beets, sweet potato and other tuber type ground vegetables. Grains were rice, corn, and wheat. Meats were poultry, oxen and pork.

For the Chinese Shar-Pei I recommend foods that blend horse meat, poultry, beet pulp, wheat and rice. These should be high in their fiber and carbohydrate content. I also suggest that you avoid feeding a Chinese Shar-Pei any avocado, white or red potatoes, ocean fish, beef or lamb.

CHOW CHOW

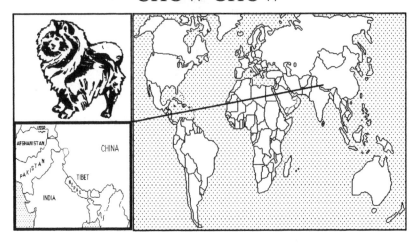

Weight Standards: m/f - average 70 lbs.
Height Standards: m/f - average 20 inches
Coat: long, dense, double, single color
Common Ailments: hot spots, eye problems, ear infections

The Chow Chow originated in China (Tibet) where it was raised as a meat source for human consumption. This was done on a scale that can be compared to the sheep ranches of New Zealand or the cattle ranches in our own country today.

Since the Chow Chow was used as a meat source for human consumption, it was fed a diet of grains and vegetables. One indicator of the Chow Chow's development as a vegetarian is the difference in the mouth, jaw, and tooth structure from those breeds that developed as "meat eaters." For example, the Chow has a set of teeth that are flatter than the sharp incisors found in the carnivorous breeds.

The Chow has two other distinctive physical features that are unique to this breed of dog; first, a blue-black tongue, and second, a lack of angulation in the lower joint of the hindlimbs.

The primary food sources of the Chow Chow's native environment were rice, wheat, soy, and some occasional fish. Thus, a blend of these foods would be the ideal diet for the Chow Chow. Conversely, the worst blend would contain beef, horse meat, lamb, and poultry or any of their by-products.

CLUMBER SPANIEL

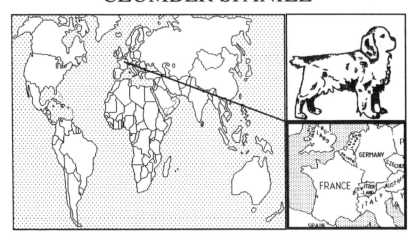

Weight Standards: m - 70 to 85 lbs., f - 65 to 75 lbs.
Height Standards: m/f - 17 to 18 inches
Coat: short & wavy with longer feathering, white or lemon colors
Common Ailments: dysplasia, skin rashes and ear ailments

The Clumber Spaniel developed prior to the French Revolution (1789) on the estate of a French nobleman, the *Duc de Noialles*. During the Revolution these dogs were taken to the Clumber Park Estate of the English *Duke of Newcastle*, who was a fancier of the breed and a friend of the *Duc de Noialles*. It was from the kennels on the English estate that the breed became popular. The breed bears its present name to honor their English Clumber Park home. This is the largest of the spaniels and their size is a definite nutritional factor when compared to other breeds. Most of their body weight is due to muscle fiber, which is heavier than fat on a square inch basis. Due to this feature they can store more protein for energy use than many retrievers that need high carbohydrate diets to fuel quick energy bursts for use during a hunt.

Native food supplies for this breed would have been poultry of the game variety (chukker, quail etc.) and meats such as venison and mutton. The vegetables of their native environment would have been potatoes and cabbage and the grains would have been flax, wheat and corn.

For the Clumber Spaniel I recommend foods with a blend of poultry, lamb, potato, wheat, and yellow corn. However, I feel you should avoid feeding a food containing white rice, fish, beef, or horse meat by-products to this breed.

COLLIE

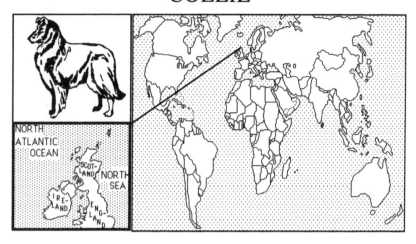

Weight Standards: m - 60 to 75 lbs., f - 50 to 60 lbs.
Height Standards: m - 24 to 26 inches, f - 22 to 24 inches
Coat: Long dense, straight outer coat-double coated with
a very heavy undercoat. Blows coat 2-3 times a year normally
Common Ailments: collie eye (detached retina), skin-coat problems

The Collie originated in the Scottish Highlands as a herding dog for both sheep and cattle. First written about in the 14th century, it received its name from the type of animals with which it associated. Black faced sheep were called "Colleys"; therefore the dogs that drove them to market were called the "Colley dogs."

The Collie has high requirements for both the mineral complex and fat soluble vitamins per pound of body weight when compared to many other breeds. .Fleischman laboratories established their vitamin D requirement in 1944. The Fleischman laboratories test shows the Collie to have a requirement for this one fat soluble vitamin over 9 times what other breeds require. The National Research Council used this report when they were considering the minimum amounts to recommend for all breed dog food. The report is cited on page 24, in the U.S. Government National Research Council publication <u>Nutrient Requirements of Dogs</u>, (1985 revised edition),

The Collie thrives on a diet that is rich in low ground type vegetables. The ideal meat protein blend should include lamb and poultry with a limited amount of beef. Collies should avoid foods containing yellow corn, rice, fish or soy.

COTON DE TULEAR

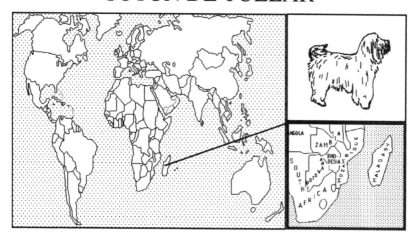

Weight Standards: m/f - 12 to 15 lbs.
Height Standards: m/f - 10 to 12 inches
Coat: long, and with the feel of cotton; color varies from white, white with champagne highlights, and a dusting of black hairs to white with black patches.
Common Ailments: skin rashes, tooth loss & respiratory problems

The Coton de Tulear developed in Madagascar, which is now the Malagasy Republic. This is an island republic located about 250 miles off the African coast in the Indian Ocean. The Coton de Tulear is called the "Royal Dog of Madagascar" because it was once owned exclusively by the royal family of the island. On the island anyone else found with a dog of this breed in their possession risked being sentenced to death. Due to the original restrictions on the breeding and ownership of this breed, it remains today one of the world's rarest breeds.

Native food supplies found in Madagascar for this breed would have been similar to brown rice, goat, fish, pork and poultry.

For the Coton de Tulear I recommend a food that is a blend of brown rice, fish, avocado and poultry. I also suggest that you keep foods such as beef or horse meat out of their diet.

CURLY COATED RETRIEVER

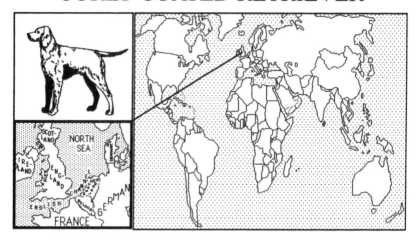

Weight Standards: m/f - average 65 lbs.
Height Standards: m/f - average 23.5 inches
Coat: short and very curly, in colors of solid liver or black
Common Ailments: dysplasia, liver and kidney failure

The Curly Coated Retriever developed in the 16th century as both an upland game dog and water retriever. An English sportsman used two breeds of Spaniel and a retrieving Setter to produce the Curly Coated Retriever we now know. It has an extremely steady temperament and is very good around children. As a retriever, it has a very tender mouth that will not damage the game. The Curly Coated Retriever is now the most popular retriever in both New Zealand and Australia.

Native food supplies for this breed and its forefathers would have been upland game birds, such as chukker and quail, and waterfowl, such as duck and goose. Grain crops of wheat and corn grew in this environment. These grains are still used by sportsmen today to attract wild game birds along their flyway.

For the Curly Coated Retriever I recommend foods that consist of poultry and wheat. The best blend for this breed should contain very high amounts of the poultry fat. I also recommend you avoid feeding any food that contains any beef, soy or white rice to a Curly Coated Retriever.

DACHSHUND

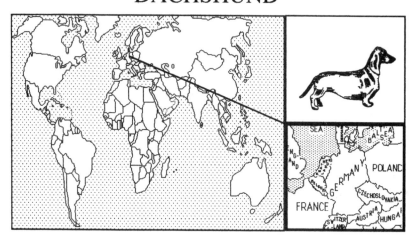

Weight Standards: m/f -16 to 22 lbs. (miniature 10 to 12 lbs.)
Height Standards: m/f - 9 to 10 inches, (miniature ± 5 inches)
Coat: three different coat types;
1) long and soft, 2) short and soft, 3) wire haired.
Common Ailments: spinal disk problems

The Dachshund originated in Germany as a hunting dog. They worked in packs and are keen nosed and tenacious in pursuit of their quarry. The specific part of Germany where they developed had rocky foothills housing wild boar and burrowing animals like badger and ground rodents. The Dachshund's long low body was ideal for going into the tunnel homes of this type of quarry.

The area in Germany this breed can call home also produced many varieties of vegetables such as potatoes, cabbage, carrots, and greens. Nutrients from these vegetable sources have high amounts of fat soluble vitamins such as vitamin A as beta carotene; therefore, I feel today's Dachshund will do best on a diet with its vitamin A source being the molecular structure of beta carotene instead of palmitate or fish oil.

Many breeders claim the Dachshund requires a very high fat - low protein ratio in their food. I feel the best food blend for the Dachshund will contain horse meat, wheat, yellow corn, and beef. The food sources to avoid with this breed include beet pulp, soy, and both the white and brown forms of rice.

DALMATIAN

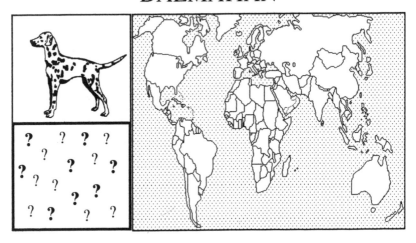

Weight Standards: m - 55 to 65 lbs., f - 45 to 55 lbs.
Height Standards: m/f - 19 to 23 inches
Coat: short and fine in white with black or liver spots
Common Ailments: cataracts, skin rashes, hot spots, liver and kidney failure, deafness related to nerve impulse blockage

The Dalmatian has been known world wide since the Middle Ages. The largest numbers of them are located in Central Europe and the British Islands Theories about the origins of this breed are numerous. The two most popular theories are that they developed either in Hungary or in Africa. Because of their coat, I would guess the warmer climate of Africa.

Due to a Dalmatian fancier who was a friend, this was the first breed that came to my attention as having nutritional requirements different from other breeds of dogs. This is also a breed I cite when asked about the length of time it takes a dog to adapt to nutrients different from those found in its native environment. The Dalmatian has remained the same world wide for many centuries. Yet the ailments suffered by this one breed vary from one area to the next. I feel the different ailments suffered are a direct result of this one breed's exposure to different environmental food supplies.

Today's Dalmatian seems to do best when fed a blend of lamb, poultry, and white rice. Foods that seem to give this breed the most problems will contain soy, beef, or horse meat by-products, and high fiber products like wheat, oats, and yellow corn.

DANDIE DINMONT TERRIER

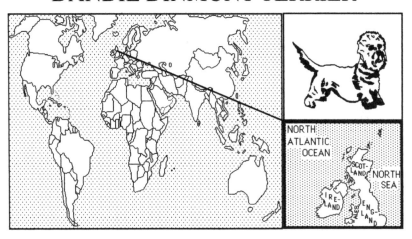

Weight Standards: m/f - 18 to 24 lbs.
Height Standards: m/f - 8 to 12 inches
Coat: medium long & rough textured, in mustard or peppered color
Common Ailments: kidney & liver failure, slipped stifle, and ear infections

The Dandie Dinmont Terrier developed in the border country between England and Scotland. The first written report of this breed, in the early 1700's, described a mustard colored ratter and hunting dog used for otter and badger. They became popular and were renamed after Sir Walter Scott published the novel Guy Mannering in 1814. One character in the novel, Dandie Dinmont, owned a pack of pepper and mustard colored terriers. Sir Walter Scott described the dogs in such glowing terms that the pepper or mustard colored terriers of the north country became very popular throughout the British Empire. When the breed was registered in 1876 it bore the name Dandie Dinmont Terrier.

Native food supplies for this breed came from the rocky soil of the border country and consisted of meats from rodent, otter, badger, and poultry. Vegetable crops were cabbage, potato, and carrots.

For the Dandie I recommend a blend of poultry, horse meat, fish, and potato carbohydrates You should avoid feeding a Dandie any food blends that contain soy, yellow corn, or beet pulp.

DOBERMAN PINSCHER

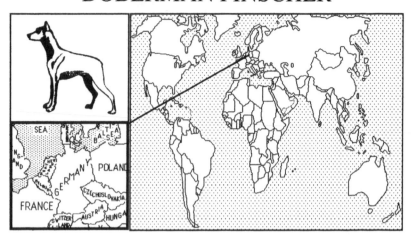

Weight Standards: m - 70 to 75 lbs., f - 60 to 65 lbs.
Height Standards: m - 26 to 28 inches, f - 24 to 26 inches
Coat: short and smooth in black with tan or red
Common Ailments: circulatory problems, cold sensitive,
bloat and kidney failure

The Doberman Pinscher originated in the shadows of Germany's beer breweries. Today the Dobe is internationally renowned as a security dog. It has an extremely high degree of loyalty to its master and can be very territorial, yet its temperament also makes it good with children.

The Doberman Pinscher needs a special blend to receive good bio-nutritive value from protein. When compared to other breeds of the same body weight, it requires higher amounts of certain amino acids. The protein should be high in Phenylalanine and Thyrosine. Since the bulk nutrients of the area where the Doberman Pinscher developed were high in these essential amino acids, this breed requires this same protein blend today. Food sources found in the Doberman Pinscher's native environment included grain crops used for brewing German beer with pork and beef meat sources.

The protein sources I feel would be the best for this breed of dog are a blend of beef, corn, wheat, and horse meat. Conversely, the worst blend would contain high amounts of poultry, ocean fish, or white rice.

ENGLISH COCKER SPANIEL

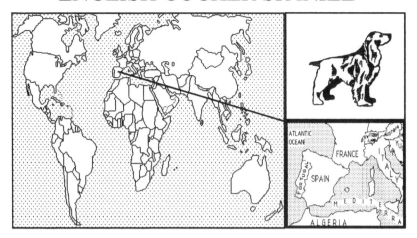

Weight Standards: m - 28 to 34 lbs., f - 26 to 32 lbs.
Height Standards: m - 16 to 17 inches, f - 15 to 16 inches
Coat: flat, long and wavy in a variety of colors
Common Ailments: hot spots and other skin and coat problems

The English Cocker Spaniel can trace its origins to Spain just like most of the other "Spaniel" breeds. The breed became popular in the 14th century when imported to England as a woodland bird hunting dog. The woodland bird that this spaniel hunted was the Woodcock, commonly called a "Cocker"; therefore, this breed became known as a Cocker Spaniel. The English Cocker has a harder time adapting to food changes than does the American Cocker. We also see more obvious reactions to food allergies with this breed than their American relative. In this country the English Cocker suffers from many skin allergies that are not commonly found within the breed in their native England. I feel this is due to the water differences between these two areas compounded by the differences in mineral sources present in most commercial foods from these two countries.

Native food supplies for this breed would have been very high in carbohydrate content. They included potatoes with other starchy vegetables, grains blended with meats from poultry (woodcock and other upland game birds), and mutton.

For the English Cocker I recommend foods that contain poultry, lamb wheat, oats, and potato. Also the minerals should be from a gluconate form and not a sulfate source. I recommend that you avoid feeding an English Cocker soy, ocean fish, beef, or yellow corn.

109

ENGLISH FOXHOUND

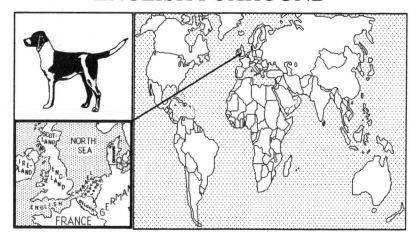

Weight Standards: m/f - 70 to 75 pounds
Height Standards: m - 24 inches, f - 23 inches
Coat: short and smooth yet very thick, in white with black
and brown tricolor
Common Ailments: hot spots and liver failure

The **English Foxhound** developed through very selective breeding on the hunting estates of England's upper crust. The breed has always been used for one purpose; that of running down the fox ahead of horsemen. They are a very lean and muscular breed. This physical characteristic of body fat to muscle tissue ratio is a nutritional factor that needs to be considered when looking at their food requirements. They can store large amounts of protein to supply their energy requirements during the hunt. They also require large quantities of water during this exercise.

Food supplies for this breed included the fox, hare, and other small animals from their native environment combined with the type of vegetables and grain crops found in England's central farmlands.

For the English Foxhound I recommend foods high in their fiber content. The carbohydrates should be from sources of potato, oats, and wheat with the meats from lean horse meat and beef. I also feel you should avoid feeding an English Foxhound any ocean fish, soy, poultry, or yellow corn.

ENGLISH SETTER

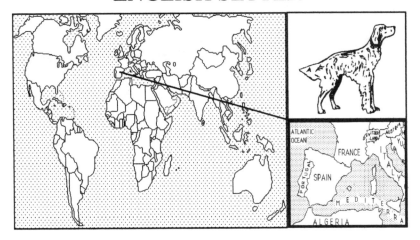

Weight Standards: m - 60 to 70 lbs., f - 50 to 60 lbs.
Height Standards: m - 25 inches, f - 24 inches
Coat: long and straight, silky, with feathering
Common Ailments: dysplasia, hot spots and kidney failure

The English Setter came to England in the 14th century from Spain. Its name comes from the way it "set" a game bird for the hunter to net. Today, most sportsmen consider this breed to be the most elegant gundog there is.

The English Setter requires large amounts of arachidonic acid. It will produce this acid through natural body functions, if fed food sources that contain certain polyunsaturated fatty acids. These must contain the proper balance of linoleic, linolenic, and oleic acids. You can tell if an English Setter is receiving the proper diet and producing the required arachidonic acid by the gloss of the coat. The best sources of the polyunsaturated fatty acids for this breed are wheat germ oil or safflower oil. The worst balance of the fatty acids for this breed would be found in sources of beef fat or soy oils.

The English Setter developed in an area of Spain that produced grain crops of wheat and brown rice, poultry (mainly game birds), and cattle. I feel the ideal diet for the English Setter is a blend of foods that are high in natural fiber with a high carbohydrate to low protein ratio. The best food blend would contain poultry, lamb, and brown rice with wheat and yellow corn. Conversely the least desirable blend would contain horse meat, fish, rice, and soy.

ENGLISH SPRINGER SPANIEL

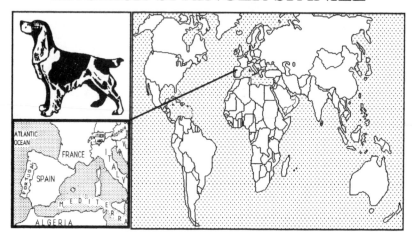

Weight Standards: m - 49 to 55 lbs., f - 44 to 50 lbs.
Height Standards: m - 20 inches, f - 19 inches
Coat: long, smooth, double, tricolored
Common Ailments: thyroid disorders, hip dysplasia

The English Springer Spaniel originated as an upland game bird hunting dog in Spain during the late 1200's and early 1300's. It was then taken to the British Islands where it completed its development into the English Springer we know today. They are named "Springer" because they were used to "spring" game for the sportsman's net and "Spaniel" because they came to England from Spain.

This breed primarily developed on a diet of corn, wheat, and fowl (such as partridge, quail, and pheasant). English Springer Spaniel owners should be aware that protein from wild poultry sources has amino acid profiles that are quite different from those of chicken by-products used in many commercial all-breed dog foods. Therefore, this breed will require more than just chicken or chicken by-products as the meat protein in its food to come close to the best amino acid balance required.

For the English Springer Spaniel I recommend a blend of corn, wheat, and lamb with chicken. The food also should be high in its poultry fat content. I also suggest that you avoid protein sources based on beet pulp or soy with beef or horse meat and their by-products for this breed.

112

ENGLISH TOY SPANIEL

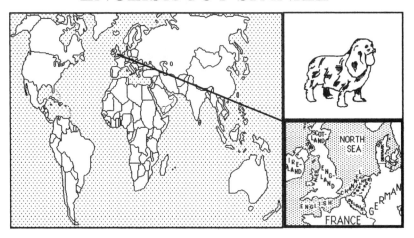

Weight Standards: m/f - 9 to 12 lbs.
Height Standards: m/f - average 9.5 inches
Coat: long soft & wavy in red, red & white, black & tan or tricolor
Common Ailments: subject to slipped stifle, eye lacerations
and respiratory problems

The English Toy Spaniel developed in England and was popular before the reign of William of Orange. It was a constant companion of the English Cocker Spaniel that developed in the same time and area. The English Toy Spaniel we know today is a product of selective breeding that took place just prior to the reign of Edward VII and bears little physical resemblance to its predecessors. In England and most of the world this breed's name is "*THE KING CHARLES SPANIEL* ". It is called "*THE TOY SPANIEL* " only in the United States and Canada. This is due to Edward VII's refusal to allow the name *Toy Spaniel* to become the registered name for this breed since it had so little in common with the other "Spaniel" breeds of England during the time of his reign.

Native food supplies for this breed would have been the same as the English Cocker. They consisted of potatoes and other starchy vegetables blended with meats from wild poultry (woodcock and other upland game birds), and mutton.

For the English Toy Spaniel I recommend foods that contain poultry, lamb, wheat, oats, and potato. I also recommend that you avoid feeding them any soy products, ocean fish, beef, or yellow corn.

113

FIELD SPANIEL

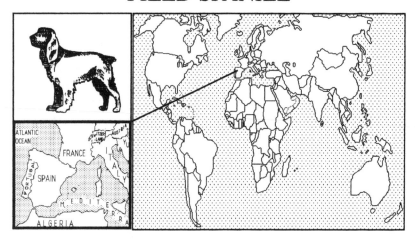

Weight Standards: m/f - 35 to 50 lbs.
Height Standards: m/f - 18 inches
Coat: short with a silky texture, in solid black, liver or mahogany
Common Ailments: dysplasia, liver and kidney failure, respiratory problems

The Field Spaniel has a history that closely resembles that of the English Cocker Spaniel. Its forefathers came to England from Spain, and English breeders developed it for hunting upland game birds. Today's Field Spaniel has gained respect of dog fanciers and is steadily gaining in popularity. However, at one time the breed suffered in popularity, and today remains one of the rarest of the sporting breeds. This loss of popularity started in England because of some breeders who were originally producing the Field Spaniel. In their effort to produce a sturdier dog than the English Cocker, they indiscriminately bred a dog with a number of negative traits. Concerned breeders removed these negative traits in later generations. Today's Field Spaniel is a well balanced and desirable hunting companion.

Native food supplies for this breed would have been woodcock, chukker, quail, pheasant, and other upland game birds combined with the grain crops and vegetables found in middle latitude England.

For the Field Spaniel I recommend foods that have a blend of wheat, oats, poultry, and lamb. However, I feel you should avoid feeding a Field Spaniel any soy, white rice, beet pulp, beef, and horse meats or their by-products.

FILA BRASILEIRO

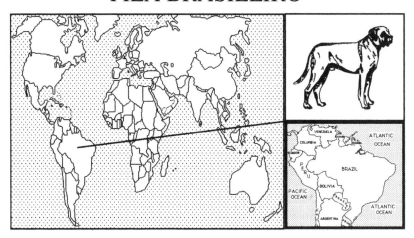

Weight Standards: m/f - over 110 lbs.
Height Standards: m - 27 to 29.5 inches, f - 26 to 28 inches
Coat: short and dense in any color including brindle except white
Common Ailments: dysplasia

The Fila Brasileiro developed in Brazil as the result of crossbreeding select Portuguese herding breeds with the English Mastiff. It is a very courageous dog that hunts the Jaguar. It makes a great watchdog because it is territorial and loyal. However, these same traits can cause it to be overly aggressive with strangers.

The Fila Brasileiro is a very heavy-boned breed that requires a high quantity of the mineral complex throughout its life to develop and maintain its skeletal structure. Also, it is a breed that is slow to mature (nutritionally), even though it reaches its adult body size in 18 to 24 months. Therefore, it should be kept on a puppy feeding program until fully developed at about 40 months of age.

Native food supplies for this breed came from the border of the rain forest (selvas) in Brazil. These included cattle, sheep, mango Papaya, and brown rice.

For the Fila Brasileiro I recommend foods that are high in their fiber content and have the meat sources from a beef and lamb blend. The food also should contain avocado, beet pulp, and brown rice. However, I feel you should avoid feeding this breed any poultry, white rice, or soy products.

115

FLAT-COATED RETRIEVER

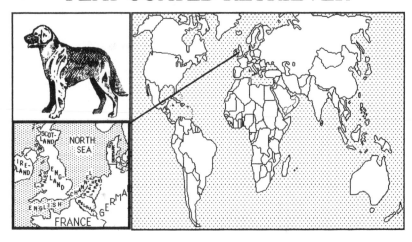

Weight Standards: m/f - 60 to 70 lbs.
Height Standards: m/f - 23 inches
Coat: soft with mild feathering, black in color
Common Ailments: hot spots, dysplasia

The Flat-Coated Retriever we know today developed as a result of dog fancier S.E. Shirley's efforts. S.E. Shirley lived in England and was also the founder of The Kennel Club of England in 1873. The breeds that Shirley used to develop the Flat-Coated Retriever were the Labrador Retriever, the St. Johns Newfoundland, and the Collie. In the late 1800's and early 1900's the Flat-Coated Retriever was one of the most popular show dogs in Britain. It has a wonderful temperament and is good in the home with children as well as being an excellent water retriever and field dog.

When we are tracing the nutrients that would have played a role in this relatively new breed's development, we must consider its forefather's native food supplies. The native food supplies for each of these are listed in the chapters that pertain to the Flat-Coated's forefathers; the Labrador Retriever, the St. Johns Newfoundland and the Collie.

For the Flat-Coated Retriever I recommend foods that are a blend of poultry, fish, wheat, oats, and yellow corn. However, I also recommend that you avoid feeding a Flat-Coated Retriever any soy products, beet pulp, and any red meats with low fat content.

116

FOX TERRIER

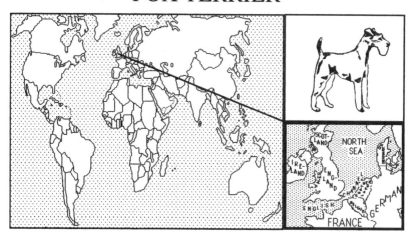

Weight Standards: m - average 18 lbs., f - average 16 lbs.
Height Standards: m/f - less than 15.5 inches
Coat: two types: Smooth variety - short, fine textured and smooth.
Wirehaired variety - short, extremely dense and wiry (this type
needs stripping). Both found in white with black, ginger or tan
Common Ailments: nasal problems (drip), hot spots, hyperthyroid

The Fox Terrier comes in two varieties. Both varieties of this one
breed developed in England to hunt fox. They were first written about
in the 18th century as able hunters that could "gallop and stay and follow
their fox up a drain." To put this in lay terms, it means the Fox Terrier
could keep up with the hounds and horse while it had a fox on the run.
It then (because of its body size) could follow the fox into a hole to chase
it out for the hunter. Both the smooth and wire varieties of this breed
have been in the show ring in the United States for over 100 years.
Because of their history as a hunting dog, Fox Terriers were shown in
the sporting breed group. They were recently placed with the terrier
group.

Native food supplies for both varieties of this breed would have been the
grain crops of England; those that would grow in the rocky soil in a
damp climate, and meats from the fox, badger and other borough land
game they hunted.

For the Fox Terrier I recommend foods that contain beef, horse meat,
and grains of oats, wheat, and yellow corn. However, I also recommend
you avoid feeding a Fox Terrier any ocean variety of fish, soy, or white
rice.

FRENCH BULLDOG

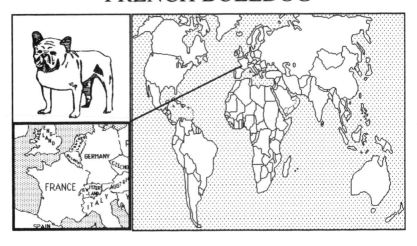

Weight Standards: m/f - under 28 lbs.
Height Standards: m/f - average 11.5 inches
Coat: short and smooth, in brindle, fawn or white
Common Ailments: eye and respiratory problems

The French Bulldog, *Bouldouge Francais* , was developed in France by a group of lace workers who emigrated from Nottingham, England. The dog that they brought with them was a toy sized English Bulldog. They selectively bred these to local dogs that had a unique head and ear shape. The results of this breeding program gave us a small breed with the classic body of a Bulldog and a unique domed shaped skull. The skull has a domed appearance because of its flatness between the ears and a slight curvature directly above the eyes. The ears are "bat ear" in shape and give the French Bulldog a quaint and inquiring look.

Native food supplies for this breed would have been found in both the areas of Nottingham, England (located on the banks of the Trent River) and Central France. The grain crops of both areas are very similar with sugar beets being abundant. The other main crops are wheat, oats, and barley. The meat from both areas is also similar. It is from beef and dairy cattle raised for both tilling and food.

For the French Bulldog I recommend foods that are a blend of beef, wheat, oats, and beet pulp. However, I feel you should avoid feeding a French Bulldog any soy products, avocado, or white rice.

GERMAN SHEPHERD DOG

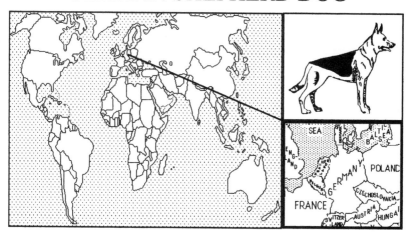

Weight Standards: m - 80 to 85 lbs., f - 65 to 70 lbs.
Height Standards: m - 24 to 26 inches, f - 22 to 24 inches
Coat: dense, straight, short, tricolored
Common Ailments: dysplasia, and gastric disorders

The German Shepherd Dog originated in the Alsatian Region of Germany. Today it is used world wide as a sentry, police dog, tracker, drug dog, search and rescue dog, and guide dog for the blind. The official name for this breed is *German Shepherd Dog*, though it is often called the German Shepherd or just Shepherd. For many years this was the only breed shown at AKC shows within the U.S.A. that had the word *dog* in its official name.

The German Shepherd Dog is unique because it has a very short colon in comparison to other breeds of the same body weight. For this reason a high fiber diet is required to slow the movement of food through this breed's digestive track, thereby allowing more time for the nutrients to be drawn out. This high fiber diet will result in a larger stool but better assimilation of the food. I caution that this fiber must be from the proper sources and the amount should be carefully controlled. Too much fiber or fiber of the wrong type can cause impacted bowels.

The environment for the Alsatian Region of Germany provided this breed with primary food sources of beef, wheat, and leafy greens like cabbage and alfalfa. Thus, I recommend a blend of these food sources as the ideal base diet for the German Shepherd. Conversely, I feel the worst food blend for the German Shepherd Dog would contain fish, soy, or rice.

GERMAN SHORTHAIRED POINTER

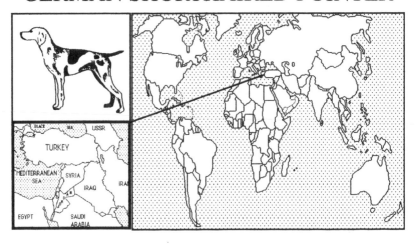

Weight Standards: m - 55 to 70 lbs., f - 45 to 60 lbs.
Height Standards: m - 23 to 25 inches, f - 21 to 23 inches
Coat: short, single, smooth, liver and white
Common Ailments: Dysplasia, an overeater

The German Shorthaired Pointer can trace its origins to the 12th Century city of Constantinople. This city is now called Istanbul and is in today's country of Turkey. This breed is an all-purpose gun dog developed for the sportsman who wanted a companion that could hunt either fur or feather on land or water.

The nutritional environment of 12th Century Constantinople would have provided meats of poultry, goat, and fish. The fruits would have included the fig, grape, orange, and olive. The predominant grains of the area were barley, a brown rice and wheat. This nutritional combination played a major role in determining the dietary requirements of the German Shorthaired Pointer. One result was that this breed developed a requirement for a high fat and oil content in its food from vegetable oils. Another is its need for proteins that are high in methionine (from the types of fruit named), and leucine and lysine (from the fish and poultry meat sources).

I recommend you use a food that contains a blend of poultry, fish, lamb, avocado, and wheat for this breed. I also recommend you avoid blends that contain beef by-products, soy, yellow corn, and beet pulp for a German Shorthaired Pointer.

GERMAN WIREHAIRED POINTER

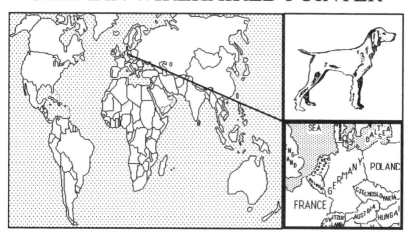

Weight Standards: m - 60 to 75 lbs., f - 50 to 60 lbs.
Height Standards: m - 24 to 26 inches, f - not under 22 inches
Coat: double, top coat short, dense and wiry in liver & white
Common Ailments: bloat, gas and other intestinal tract problems

The German Wirehaired Pointer developed in Northern Germany because sportsmen wanted both a water retriever and a pointer of upland game-birds. This breed is a very heavy shedder in the warmer summer months. This seasonal shedding is a nutritional factor that should be considered in their dietary requirements. Since their coat's fiber is made from protein, their protein requirements change when it comes time to grow their winter coat. I suggest an increase in their dietary protein during the fall months to help produce the heavier new winter coat. The increase in the dietary protein content should be about 2% to 3% above their normal maintenance diet. This can be achieved by feeding them a commercial formula with the same base sources as in their everyday food, but with a higher protein amount. Note; Many puppy formulas would meet these changes. Once the new coat is set, they can then return to lower protein food for the balance of the year.

Native food supplies for this breed would have been poultry of the game bird variety, mutton, pork, and fresh water fish. Also available was wheat with other high carbohydrate / starchy vegetables like cabbage and potato.

For the German Wirehaired Pointer I recommend a blend of poultry, lamb, wheat, potato, and fish. I also recommend you avoid feeding a soy and white rice blend to a German Wirehaired Pointer.

GIANT SCHNAUZER

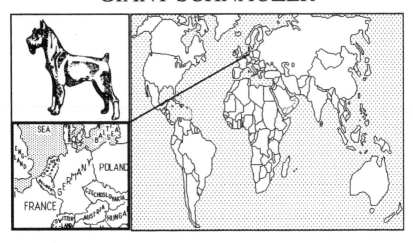

Weight Standards: m - 75 to 95 lbs., f - 75 to 85 lbs.
Height Standards: m - 25.5 to 27.5 inches, f - 23.5 to 25.5 inches
Coat: double coated, short, dense, very harsh texture with leg
and chin feathering in solid black or salt and pepper
Common Ailments: dysplasia and bloat

The Giant Schnauzer developed in the German kingdoms of Wurttenberg and Bavaria where this dog was known as a "Muncher" in the early 15th century. The original development of this breed was from a line of the smaller Standard Schnauzers. German meat packers selectively bred these dogs to a larger size dog that could both herd and guard. A special note: this breed's skeletal system is not fully developed until about 36 months of age, even though a 12 month old puppy may have reached a full adult body size. Therefore, as with other breeds that are slow to develop nutritionally, this breed must be kept on a puppy diet until fully developed both internally as well as externally.

Native food supplies for this breed would have included the type of grains used in the German breweries such as hops and flax with ground vegetables such as potato and cabbage. Also wheat and sugar beet were grown for the herds of beef cattle with which this breed associated.

For the Giant Schnauzer I recommend foods that have beef as their meat source blended with beet and grains of wheat and corn. I also recommend that you avoid feeding a Giant Schnauzer any soy, white rice, or poultry.

GLEN OF IMAAL TERRIER

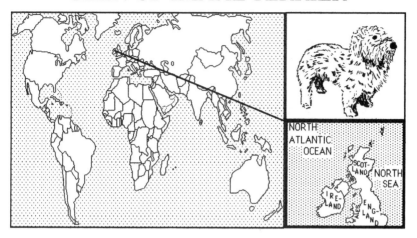

Weight Standards: m/f - up to 35 lbs.
Height Standards: m/f - 14 inches
Coat: a harsh textured coat in blue, blue and tan or Wheaton color
Common Ailments: hot spots, liver and kidney disorders

The Glen of Imaal Terrier is a true dog of Ireland, with a history that dates from 2500 BC. It is a courageous breed that originally hunted badgers in the rocky cliffs of Wicklow County on the southeast coast of Ireland. One of the things this breed does differently than other Terriers is it will not bark or make any noise when fighting - even when taking on a fox or badger in the lair. Physically this breed is very heavily boned for its size. It also has a large chest to house a set of lungs that are very large for a dog of only 14 inches and 35 pounds. I feel that both of these physical features play a role in the unique nutritional requirements of this breed.

Food supplies native to this breed would have been the ground animals it hunted. Both ocean and stream fish were a staple in its diet. The grain and vegetable crops native to Wicklow County Ireland would have included barley, oats, and potato.

For the Glen of Imaal Terrier I recommend foods that are high in the protein from a fish source blended with barley, oats, potato, and a little beef. However, you should avoid feeding a Glen of Imaal Terrier anything you would not find in an Irish Stew, such as white rice, soy beans, beets, or avocado.

GOLDEN RETRIEVER

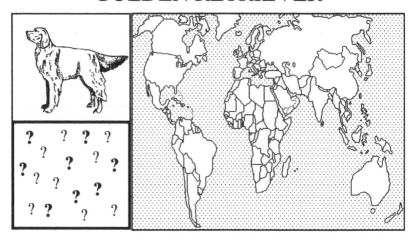

Weight Standards: m - 65 to 75 lbs., f - 60 to 70 lbs.
Height Standards: m - 23 to 24 inches, f - 21.5 to 22.5 inches
Coat: double, soft and long with mild feathering
Common Ailments: dysplasia, congenital eye defects, hot spots

The Golden Retriever's origins cannot be documented. The theories are as numerous as the breed itself. One theory claims the Golden Retriever originated in Russia and was then later taken to England where it developed into the breed of dog we know today.

The Golden is one of six breeds I know of that produces oils through the skin and no skin dander. This makes it an ideal breed for people with allergies to the skin dander produced by most of the other breeds. Since the Golden produces skin oil and not skin dander, it is very important that they receive the proper amount and balance of dietary fatty acids. When the proper balance of fatty acids (linolenic, linoleic, and oleic) are present in its daily dietary intake, the Golden only produces the arachidonic acid its body requires to make the skin oils. The proper source and balance of these fatty acids can change a dry, dull and brittle coat into one that would make any Golden Retriever proud. The best sources of fatty acids for this breed of dog are linseed oil and cold pressed corn oil or wheat germ oils. Soy oil coat conditioners should be avoided.

Wherever the Golden Retriever originated, nutrient sources in the regions must have included wheat, corn, poultry, and limited amounts of beef. A blend of these sources makes up the ideal base diet for this breed. Foods this breed should avoid would contain ocean fish, soy, oats, beet pulp, or white rice.

GORDON SETTER

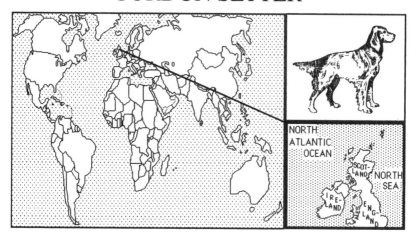

Weight Standards: m - 55 to 80 lbs., f - 45 to 75 lbs.
Height Standards: m - 24 to 27 inches, f - 23 to 26 inches
Coat: long, smooth, double with very light feathering
Common Ailments: dysplasia and hot spots

The Gordon Setter is the only breed of dog called "Setter" originating in Scotland. The Duke of Gordon developed this specific breed at the kennels on his estate. He developed it to be both a working and hunting dog. They herded sheep and pointed to feathered game for sportsmen. This combination was ideal for gentlemen who needed a working dog for most of the week and a good hunting companion for the week end.

The Gordon Setter has a special need for a high fat content diet. This need for additional dietary fat is especially high when the setter is working or when it is under stress. Large quantities of water must accompany the additional dietary fat intake during these times. A sure sign that the dog requires additional fat in its dietary intake is a brittle coat. When the Gordon has the proper amount of fat in the diet, its coat is very soft. The best sources of fats for this breed are vegetable or poultry fats. The worst source of fat for the Gordon Setter is beef fat.

The Gordon Setter's native environment in Scotland provided food sources of potatoes, wheat, corn, and poultry of the wild game variety. Therefore, I recommend a blend of foods that are high in their carbohydrate-to-protein ratio as the ideal diet for the Gordon Setter. The blend I recommend would contain potatoes, wheat, corn, and poultry. Conversely, I feel the worst blend would be white rice, soy, beef, or horse meat and their by-products.

125

GREAT DANE

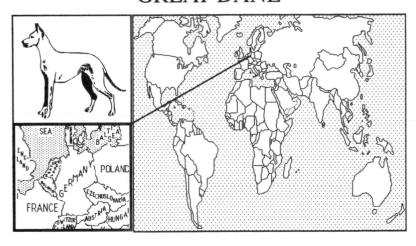

Weight Standards: m - 135 to 150 lbs., f - 120 to 135 lbs.
Height Standards: m - over 30 inches, f - over 28 inches
Coat: short, smooth with a harsh texture,
in colors of brindle, fawn, harlequin or solid black
Common Ailments: bloat, torsion, dysplasia, spinal disc problems

The Great Dane, which is called the "Apollo of Dogs", developed in Germany where they were used as a hunter and a guard dog. Their original name was "The Deutsche Dogge", and at one time they were known to be so ferocious that the breed was considered vicious. They also had earned a reputation for being an excellent war dog. They could both pack gear and protect their masters backside from attack during a battle. I note that the "breed trait" of being ferocious is no longer evident. Today the Dane is (pound for pound) one of the most gentle and loving of the species canine.

This is a breed that in its native environment is still being fed a diet of high fiber (whole rolled oats, cabbage, etc.) and high protein foods. I have seen fewer instances of bloat or torsion reported in its native Germany than I have in America. Therefore, for this special breed I recommend commercial foods that are very high in their fiber content.

The food sources found in the native environment of the Dane included high fiber whole oats, cabbage, and rye. The meats were wild boar, deer, and a lean beef from a dairy cattle. I recommend a food for today's Dane that contains beef, whole oats, rye, and potato. I also recommend that you avoid feeding a food with any soy, white rice, or fish to a Great Dane.

GREAT PYRENEES

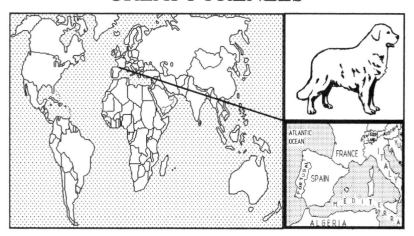

Weight Standards: m - 100 to 125 lbs., f - 90 to 100 lbs.
Height Standards: m - 27 to 32 inches, f - 25 to 29 inches
Coat: double with heavy undercoat, long soft solid white top coat
Common Ailments: dysplasia, hot spots and skin rashes,
liver and kidney failure

The Great Pyrenees developed in the Pyrenees mountains, on the border between France and Spain. This breed is one of the oldest domesticated breeds of dog with a history that has been traced to the Bronze Age (3500 to 4000 BC.). At that time it was used in its native environment for much the same purpose that it is used today; that of living in harmony with large flocks of sheep while protecting them from the bears and wolves. They possess great stamina, a keen sense of danger, and good fighting abilities.

Due to its growing popularity, the Great Pyrenees Club of America has a code of ethics clause. Members will guarantee any puppy they sell to be free from hereditary defects to protect this breed. I applaud these people in their efforts to provide us with good and healthy dogs.

Native food supplies for this breed would have been from their Pyrenees Mountain environment. The meat sources contained a very high fat to protein ratio. Any grains or vegetables would have been the type that could grow in a short season and rocky soil.

For the Great Pyrenees I recommend foods of lamb, poultry, wheat, and potato. It must have a high fat content. I also recommend you avoid feeding a food that contains soy, beef or beef by-products, yellow corn, or beet pulp to this breed.

127

GREATER SWISS MOUNTAIN DOG

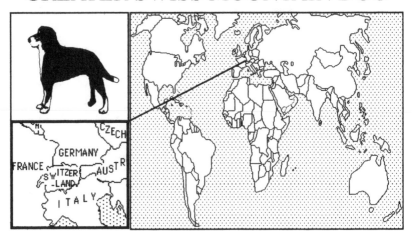

Weight Standards: m/f - 120 to 140 lbs.
Height Standards: m/f - 25 to 28 inches
Coat: double, thick long topcoat, black with bronze & white
Common Ailments: dysplasia, bloat, hot spots,
kidney and liver problems

The Greater Swiss Mountain Dog developed in the mountains of Switzerland in Central Europe. They have a history that dates from the time of Julius Caesar. They were draft dogs, herding dogs, watch dogs, and even battle companions. Nicknamed the "Swissy", it is one of four breeds known as the *Swiss Sennenhunde* (the four being the Swissy, Bernese Mountain Dog, Entlebucher, and Appenzeller). The Greater Swiss Mountain Dog is a very thick boned and heavily muscled animal, which can develop slower than other breeds. The thick bones and heavy muscles contribute to this breed's unique nutritional requirements. Therefore, the Swissy should be kept on a diet that will provide the proper nutrients for the development of bone and muscle tissue until fully developed. This can be long after the breed has reached its exterior adult body size.

Native food supplies for this breed would have been from the mountain environment of the Swiss Alps. These consisted of mutton, poultry, goat, goat dairy products, and grains of wheat, oat, and corn.

For the Greater Swiss Mountain Dog I recommend foods that contain poultry, lamb, wheat, oats, and corn. However, I feel you should avoid feeding a food that contains any ocean fish, citrus fruits or avocado, white rice, or soy products to this breed.

GREYHOUND

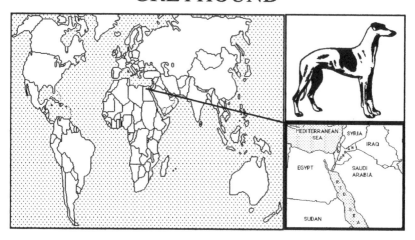

Weight Standards: m - 65 to 75 lbs., f - 60 to 65 lbs.
Height Standards: m/f - 27 to 28 inches
Coat: short, single, smooth
Common Ailments: bloat, PRA, circulatory problems

The Greyhound originated in Egypt as a hunting dog and companion to the Pharaoh and his royal family. This Egyptian desert dog is depicted inside the pyramids of many Pharaohs. Most of us know of this breed because of its performance at the race track. However, it should be noted they make wonderful family companions, as long as they have the room to exercise.

The Greyhound has unique circulatory problems directly related to its requirement for vitamins A, D, E, the mineral Selenium, and the trace mineral complex. The protein to fat requirements of this breed are very low when compared to other breeds of the same body weight. The fat should come from a vegetable or poultry source since those have the best balance for the Greyhound.

Meat sources from their native area would have consisted of rabbit, pork, poultry, and goat. Fruits would have included the fig, grape, orange, and olive. Grains were barley, wheat, and a form of brown rice.

There is no commercial food blend available in the U.S. that I would recommend for this breed. I applaud the trainers and handlers of the racing kennels for their efforts to make their own dog food. Food sources I think should be avoided by Greyhounds are beef by-products, soy, yellow corn, or beet pulp.

HARRIER

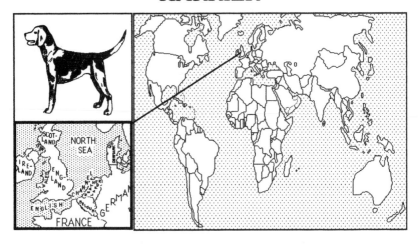

Weight Standards: m - 45 to 60 lbs., f - 40 to 55 lbs.
Height Standards: m/f - 19 to 21 inches
Coat: short and smooth in white with black and tan
Common Ailments: kidney failure, hot spots

The Harrier that we know today developed in England in the early 1200's and has one of the cleanest family tree records of any hound. Since there is an occasional puppy born with unusual coat coloring, there is a debate about the origins of the breed prior to the time records were kept on the first pack of Harriers. For five centuries we know this breed's breeding was confined to one pack, owned by a single family. The Virginia Colonial hunters used this excellent scent hound for tracking bear, boar and deer before we became a nation. They work well in a pack when hunting and have gained a good deal of respect from hunters in the southern states for their good nose and tenacity.

Native food supplies that were available to this breed in their developing years would have been meats from fox, deer, and boar. Primary vegetables were the low ground type and grains were rye and wheat.

For the Harrier I recommend foods that are a blend of horse meat, beef, and small amounts of poultry blended with wheat, oats, and yellow corn. I also recommend that you avoid feeding a Harrier any fish, beet pulp, soy, or white rice.

IBIZAN HOUND

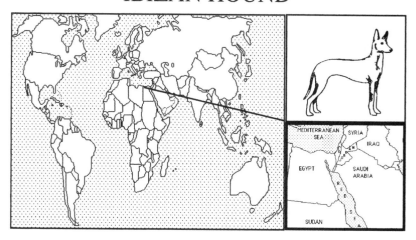

Weight Standards: m/f - 45 to 75 lbs.
Height Standards: m/f - 25 to 29 inches
Coat: short with a course texture in solid white or white with red
Common Ailments: hot spots and skin rashes

The Ibizan Hound originated in the desert regions of the Middle East. The Earliest records we have of the Ibizan Hound come from the tomb of the Egyptian Pharaoh *Tutankhamen.* This breed was also known as the *Galgo* during the time of the Pharaohs. Egyptian gods and mortals such as Cleopatra considered it a favorite. Phoenician traders were responsible for this dog's likeness being placed on the Roman coins. They are also given credit for transporting this breed to the island of Ibiza in the early 8th century. There, this breed remained isolated from other dog breeds and was bred pure for centuries. It is from this small Balearic island that we have today's Ibizan Hound.

Native food supplies for this breed would have been from their 8th century Balearic island home. They would have consisted of fish, rabbit, and goat meat with grains of wheat and a type of brown rice.

For the Ibizan Hound I recommend foods that are a blend of poultry, lamb, brown rice and wheat. However, you should avoid feeding an Ibizan Hound any food that contains soy, beef, horse meat, potato, or white rice.

IRISH SETTER

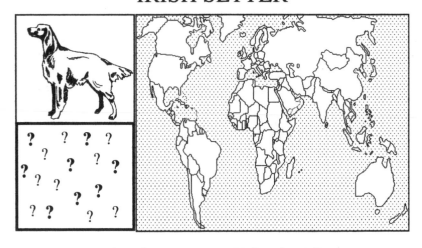

Weight Standards: m - 70 lbs.; f - 60 lbs.
Height Standards: m - 27 inches; f - 25 inches
Coat: Long, flat, silky coat with feathering, Mahogany
Common Ailments: hip dysplasia, bloat, PRA

The Irish Setter's origins remain a mystery. We do know they became popular in Ireland soon after they first appeared there a few centuries ago and that most of today's Irish Setters can trace their linage to Irish kennels. They became popular because their performance as upland bird dogs was unparalleled. They are the tallest of the setters and one of the most handsome.

The Irish Setter requires large amounts of fats, as well as a high carbohydrate to protein ratio in its base diet. It will produce a very healthy and shiny coat when the proper balance of fat-to-carbohydrate-to-protein is provided. The source of the fat in the Irish Setter's diet is very important. The best sources would be from vegetable sources and the worst would be from animal sources, such as beef fat. This is due to the different sources of fats containing different amounts and ratios of the alpha-linolenate family.

When feeding the Irish Setter, just think of the ingredients for grandma's Irish Stew. These ingredients represent the food supplies found in Ireland for centuries. I think the best food blend for the Irish Setter should contain potatoes and other vegetables such as carrots, rye grains, with meat sources of lamb and poultry. Conversely, I think the least desirable blend would contain horse meat or beef and their by-products, with soy, fish, or rice.

IRISH TERRIER

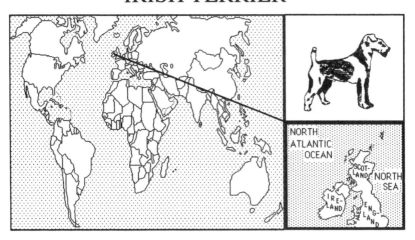

Weight Standards: m - 27 lbs., f - 25 lbs.
Height Standards: m/f - 18 inches
Coat: short with a soft undercoat and wiry top coat in shades of red
Common Ailments: kidney and liver disorders

The Irish Terrier was once known as the Irish Sporting Terrier in its native Ireland. The group of dogs collectively labeled the "Irish Sporting Terrier" included a rather mixed looking group of dogs with no breed standards. Breeders established standards after a show in Dublin, Ireland, in 1875, and the dogs conforming to these standards became the forefathers of today's Irish Terrier. The first records of this breed indicate they were a ratter and an upland game bird dog. They are very quick and agile and can catch a rabbit on the run or a woodcock before it can take wing.

Native food supplies of Ireland for this breed would have been the potato, wheat, rye, flax, game birds of the woodcock variety, fish, and mutton. So when considering the food for this breed, remember the ingredients that would have gone into Irish Stew. These ingredients represent the food supplies that have been in Ireland for centuries. Also remember the number of rice paddies you can find in Ireland is zero.

For the Irish Terrier I recommend foods containing potatoes, wheat, rye poultry, mutton (lamb), and fish. I also recommend that you avoid feeding an Irish Terrier any white rice, brown rice, avocado, or soy products.

133

IRISH WATER SPANIEL

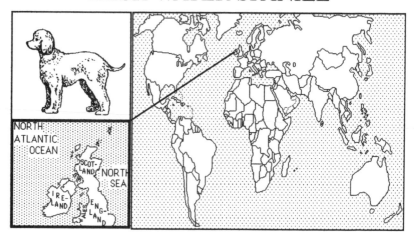

Weight Standards: m - 55 to 65 lbs., f - 45 to 58 lbs.
Height Standards: m - 22 to 24 inches, f - 21 to 23 inches
Coat: dense undercoat with a curly top coat, in liver color
Common Ailments: dysplasia, ear infections

The Irish Water Spaniel developed on the north coast of Ireland as a waterfowl retriever. Its history dates back to the 7th or 8th century. This is the tallest of the breeds called "Spaniel." The breed standards were established in 1850 after the breed gained in popularity in its native land, and local dog fanciers started promoting it. This dog is a natural retriever with a waterproof coat that makes it ideal for fetching birds brought down in extremely cold water. The Irish Water Spaniel is very territorial and protective of children given to its capable care, and yet it has a tendency to be a runner. This "running" characteristic may be to satisfy its curiosity more than to "get away from." This breed is very inquisitive, determined, and strong.

Native food supplies for this breed would have included those found in both Spain and the Northern Irish Lake Country. These included fish, waterfowl, potato, and grains of flax, rye, and oat.

For the Irish Water Spaniel I recommend foods high in their carbohydrates, with a blend of poultry, fresh water fish, potato, oats, and wheat. However, you should avoid feeding a special breed like this any soy, white rice, avocado, beef, or horse meat products.

IRISH WOLFHOUND

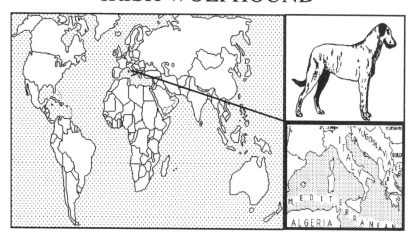

Weight Standards: m - over 120 lbs., f - over 105 lbs.
Height Standards: m - above 32 inches, f - above 30 inches
Coat: rough, short coat, gray, fawn, or brindle
Common Ailments: dysplasia, bloat & gastrointestinal problems

The Irish Wolfhound is one of the tallest of the breeds and one of the oldest. Its history can be traced to pre-Christian times when the *Legions of Rome* used it as a war dog. The Irish Wolfhound originated near Rome and was then brought to Ireland during an invasion by Roman troops. In Ireland it gained in popularity and is now their national dog. They are coveted for their hunting prowess; particularly for the pursuit and take-down of the Irish Elk, an animal that can be six feet tall at the shoulders.

Nutrients of the Irish Wolfhound's native areas were very high in carbohydrates and fiber from grain sources. The best carbohydrate food sources for the Irish Wolfhound should come from wheat, barley, and potato products. Foods with carbohydrates from sources like white rice seem to be difficult for this breed to assimilate. Irish Wolfhounds also have a lower overall protein requirement per Kg. of body weight when compared to most other breeds of dogs. Therefore, I recommend that the bulk of energy producing ingredients in this breed's diet come from fat carbohydrate sources.

My recommendation is for food with a high fiber, carbohydrate, and fat percentages. Horse meat seems to provide the best amino acid profile for this breed's requirements. I also think the Irish Wolfhound should avoid foods that contain fish, poultry, white rice, and soy.

ITALIAN GREYHOUND

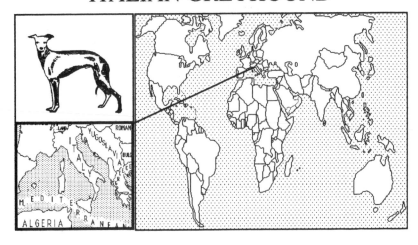

Weight Standards: m/f - average 9 lbs.
Height Standards: m/f - 13 to 15 inches
Coat: short and satin textured, any color
except tan combined with another color
Common Ailments: temperature sensitive, heart and
circulatory problems, respiratory ailments and gum disease

The Italian Greyhound originated in Italy. Roman soldiers brought it to Rome in 91 - 88 B.C.. Here it became popular and was given its modern day name. The first written word referring to this dog was uncovered in the ruins of Pompeii and was written on a plaque that read *"Cave Canem "*, which translates *"don't step on our small dog ."* This breed has experienced a decline in its life expectancy over the last century, and I blame this on the food that it is now fed. The history of the breed shows that the life span for this breed in the 16th and 17th centuries was from 15 to 17 years. This longevity is a very rare occurrence with the breed today. This breed is also prone to gum disease and tooth loss, which I also credit to nutritional factors.

Native food supplies for the Italian Greyhound would have included fruits of the citrus variety, fig and grape, brown rice, rye, wheat, and meats from hare (rabbit), goat, pork, fish, and lamb.

For the Italian Greyhound I recommend foods that are a blend of fish, poultry, lamb, brown rice, and avocado. However, I also recommend that you avoid feeding an Italian Greyhound any beef, horse meat, potato, beet pulp, or soy.

JAPANESE CHIN

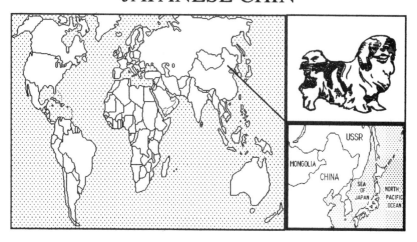

Weight Standards: m - over 7 lbs., f - under 7 lbs.
Height Standards: m/f - 12 inches
Coat: long fine overcoat in white with brown or black
Common Ailments: gum disease, respiratory, kidney & liver failure

The Japanese Chin developed in an area close to Peking, China. It was taken to the island empire of Japan in the 10th century where it became a favorite of the Emperor. It was often given as a ceremonial gift to royalty or visiting dignitaries. When Commodore Perry arrived in Japan he was given several Chins. In turn he gave his queen a breeding pair. She helped make this breed popular in England. Queen Alexandria was often painted with these small dogs in her lap or in her immediate surroundings.

This breed has a profuse coat, which is a nutritional factor in the Chin's protein requirements. To grow and maintain its thick and luxurious coat this breed can require a higher amount of protein in its food than breeds with less coat per pound of body weight.

Native food supplies for this breed would have been of the Mandarin Chinese variety with a later influence from the ocean fishing industry of Japan. These supplies would have included pork, fish, poultry with a high fat content, rice, soy products, and green's.

For the Japanese Chin I recommend foods that consist of fish, poultry, white rice, yellow corn, beet pulp, and soy. I also recommend you avoid feeding a Japanese Chin any white potato, avocado, oats, beef, or horse meat.

KEESHOND

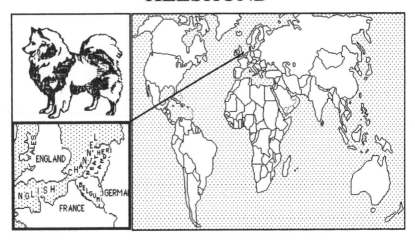

Weight Standards: m - 40 lbs., f - 35 lbs.
Height Standards: m - 18 inches, f - 17 inches
Coat: double, long stand-out top coat, silver gray shading to black
Common Ailments: hot spots and skin rash

The Keeshond, once known as the Dutch Barge Dog, originated in Holland which is now a province of the Netherlands. It served as a companion and watchdog in villages, farms, and on the canal barges. Other uses for this versatile breed of dog included hunter, herder, and draft dog.

One physical feature of the Keeshond that affects its nutritional requirements is its continuous shedding. This year round shedding creates a need for a high protein diet. I recommend dietary protein contents as high as 30% in this breed's food, as long as the protein comes from the proper sources and contains the proper balance of amino acids.

The primary food sources in the native environment of the Keeshond's low land Holland were ocean fish, dairy products, rice, beets, and poultry.

For the Keeshond I recommend blending fish and poultry protein foods that have high fatty acid contents. The foods should also have a low carbohydrate to protein ratio. The carbohydrates should be from a rice or beet pulp source. Conversely, I believe the worst food blend for a Keeshond would contain yellow corn, soy, horse meat, or lamb.

KERRY BLUE TERRIER

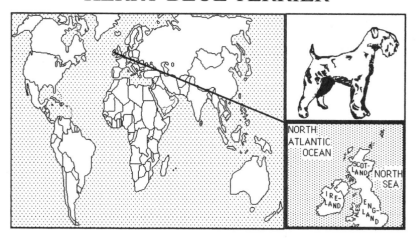

Weight Standards: m - 33 to 40 lbs., f - slightly less
Height Standards: m - 18 to 19.5 inches, f - 17.5 to 19 inches
Coat: silky textured and wavy, kept short and is blue in color
Common Ailments: skin rashes and coat pigmentation problems

The Kerry Blue Terrier, whose coat has a unique blue coloring, can trace its origins and name to County Kerry, Ireland. This county houses both Macgillycuddy's Errks and Dingle Bay and is primarily known for its fishing industry, cattle ranching, and potato farming. County Kerry, Ireland is next to County Cork on the Southwestern tip of Ireland, where it juts into the North Atlantic Ocean. The breed of dog that came from this area was an all-purpose dog. It was first used by its human companions to control the vermin population, hunt small game, and be a guard dog.

The Kerry Blue is a breed that does not shed its coat. This feature alone can make its nutritional requirements different from breeds of the same size that are heavy shedders. (See the Keeshond of Holland).

Native food supplies common to this breed's County Kerry Ireland home were rodents, beef cattle, ocean fish, and vegetables of potato, carrot, and cabbage.

For the Kerry Blue Terrier I recommend a blend of beef and fish with cabbage, carrots, and potato. You may not be able to find this combination in any commercial food. I also feel you should avoid feeding a Kerry Blue any citrus fruit, avocado, soy, or white rice.

KOMONDOR

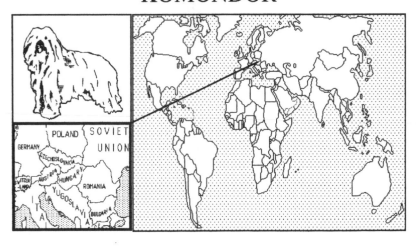

Weight Standards: m - 95 lbs., f - 80 lbs.
Height Standards: m - over 25.5 inches, f - over 23.5 inches
Coat: dense undercoat with a long "corded" top coat in solid white
Common Ailments: hip dysplasia, liver and kidney disorders

The Komondor developed in Hungary from dogs first brought to the area by Russian Magyars in the 10th century. The Komondor is quite muscular with a unique muscle to body fat ratio. This physical characteristic gives them more stamina than many other breeds of the same body weight. This is due to the muscle tissue having greater energy storing capacity than equal amounts of body fat. The Komondor's coat is also unique for two reasons: most obvious is the coat's corded appearance; however, it also has a type of fiber that can take days to dry when wet. Both physical characteristics of muscle to fat ratio and coat type are factors contributing to the Komondor's unique nutritional requirements.

Native food supplies for this breed would have been from both the steeps of Russia and later Hungary's low land farm belt. These area's are the bread basket of Europe and produce wheat, oats, barley, corn, sugar beets, hogs, and beef.

For the Komondor I recommend foods that are a blend of beef, beet pulp, yellow corn, oats, and wheat. The food should be high in its fiber content as well. I also recommend you avoid feeding a Komondor any foods containing soy, white rice, ocean fish, or avocado.

KUVASZ

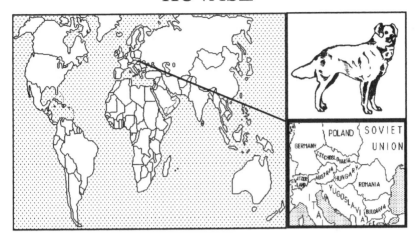

Weight Standards: m - average 80 lbs., f - average 75 lbs.
Height Standards: m - 26 inches, f - somewhat less
Coat: long top coat that is slightly wavy in white only
Common Ailments: dysplasia

The Kuvasz developed in the mountains of Hungary where it borders Czechoslovakia. This breed guarded noblemen during their journeys when it first appeared in this area in 1100 A.D.. It was later used to guard and herd flocks of sheep, and to hunt wild game. This dog has an unusually high instinct to protect children or helpless elderly. This trait makes them wonderful family pets. It is an extremely gentle dog for its size, yet it is also a strong willed herding dog. The Kuvasz's herding instinct is often used on those *they consider* in their care. They may take grandma or a small child to a place other than where they want to go. It is sometimes difficult for some people to remember that the Kuvasz does this "herding" out of love and devotion.

Native meat supplies for this breed's development would have come from their mountain environment and therefore contained high amounts of body fat. The main meat sources would have been mutton, goat, wolf, bear, and venison. The carbohydrates of their diet would have come from oats and vegetables, such as corn and beets grown in the short summer months.

For the Kuvasz I recommend foods with both the fat and protein sources from meats like mutton or poultry and not grain. You should avoid feeding a Kuvasz any foods that contain soy products (including soy "coat conditioners"), white rice, or salt water fish.

LABRADOR RETRIEVER

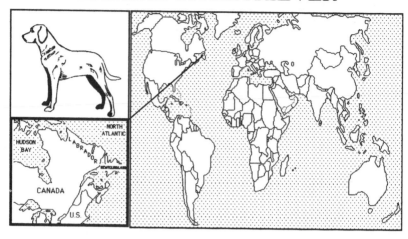

Weight Standards: m - 60 to 75 lbs., f - 55 to 70 lbs.
Height Standards: m - 22.5 to 24.5 inches, f - 21.5 to 23.5 inches
Coat: short, straight, hard, and dense; in black, yellow, or chocolate
Common Ailments: hip dysplasia, hot spots

The Labrador Retriever originated in Newfoundland and further developed in England. Besides being a famous gun dog, the Lab has become a renowned police and war dog and a trusted guide dog for the blind. The Labrador Retriever is also only one of the few breeds known to produce an oil through the pores of the skin. It will develop a very dry and brittle coat in a very short period of time when the entire Linoleic acid group is not present in its daily diet. The Linoleic acid group consist of three fatty acids: Oleic, Linolenic and Linoleic. The best commercial sources of these fatty acids for the Labrador Retriever are fish oil, linseed oil, or cold pressed wheat germ oil.

In Newfoundland the primary food sources were caribou, fish, and whale fats. In England the food sources were poultry, fish, wheat, and dairy products. The combined effect of foods from these two areas resulted in the development of a breed requiring a diet low in carbohydrates yet high in fats. The source of the fat is also important; the Labrador Retriever has a difficult time assimilating beef fat but thrives on poultry fat, fish oil, or vegetable fats.

For the Labrador Retriever I recommend foods that contain fish, poultry, lamb, and green vegetables. However, for this breed I suggest you avoid foods that are a contain beef, beets, corn, and soy.

LAKELAND TERRIER

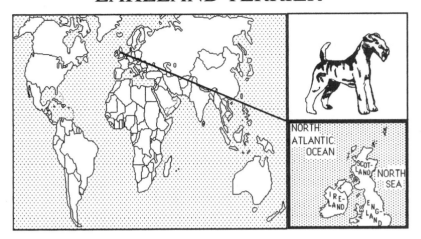

Weight Standards: m/f - 17 lbs.
Height Standards: m - 13.5 to 15.5 inches, f - 12.5 to 14 inches
Coat: a short and wiry double coat in black to Wheaton colors
Common Ailments: hot spots and skin rashes

The Lakeland Terrier developed in England's Cumberland County, a county that borders both Scotland and the Irish Sea. This county has some of the highest elevations in England, and it was from the heather moors of this region that the Lakeland Terrier originated. It was also from the many lakes in this region that the Lakeland came to be named. This breed was a working terrier. Its job was to kill fox that preyed on the farmers' new lambs and poultry. It also controlled the vermin population that lived in the storage bins and destroyed the grain. The Lakeland Terrier is tough, brave and agile, with a slender body that enables it to follow its quarry through narrow crevices. The Lakeland is also a very hardy dog that seems to adapt faster to different food sources than many other breeds.

Native food supplies for this breed would have included lamb, poultry, hare, rodent, fish, and fox with high carbohydrate starchy vegetables and grains. Vegetables and grains would have been the potato, cabbage, carrot, oats, and rye grown in the podsols/bog type of soil of their heather moors homeland.

For the Lakeland Terrier I recommend foods that are a blend of wheat, oats, lamb, poultry, and potato. However, I feel you should avoid feeding a Lakeland any soy, avocado, or other highly acidic fruits, white rice, or horse meat.

LHASA APSO

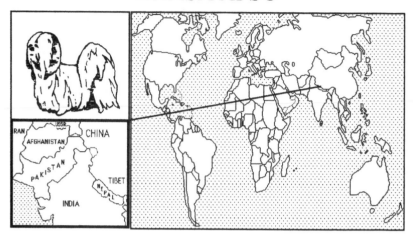

Weight Standards: m/f - 16 lbs.
Height Standards: m - 10 to 11 inches, f - slightly smaller
Coat: Long, dense straight coat, any color
Common Ailments: kidney ailments

The Lhasa Apso originated in the Himalayan Mountains of Tibet as the temple dog of the Dali Llama. Its primary function was that of a watchdog inside the palace. Its intelligence, acute hearing, and natural instinct for identifying friend from foe made the Lhasa uniquely suited for this role.

The primary meats available as a food of Tibet would have been domesticated yak, mountain goat, bear, or lama. These meats have unique amino acid profiles when compared to meats usually used in commercial all-breed dog foods within the U.S.A. Their native home environment also produced barley and rice crops, which are grains high in fiber and carbohydrates. I feel that both of these grain crops influenced the nutritional requirements of the Lhasa Apso. They still require a diet that is higher in carbohydrates and fiber than many other breeds of dog of the same body size.

Formulas that the Lhasa Apso can use blend poultry, fish, rice, soy and wheat. I also recommend you avoid feeding a Lhasa Apso foods with sources that contain any beef, yellow corn, beet pulp, or white potatoes.

MALTESE

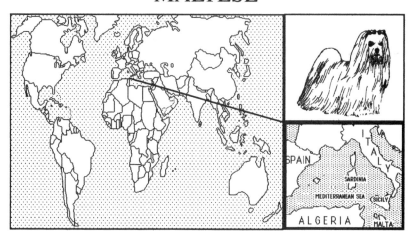

Weight Standards: m/f - under 7 lbs.
Height Standards: m/f - average 5 inches
Coat: a long straight top coat, fine textured in solid white
Common Ailments: slipped stifle, gum disease, respiratory

The Maltese developed on the islands of Malta. These islands are a small chain in the Mediterranean Sea between the coast of Sicily and the coast of Africa. The Maltese were a favorite of the Greeks. Often these dogs were a subject for Greek artists during the 5th century, and tombs were erected for deceased pet Maltese. The Maltese dogs of Malta look the same today as they appear in portraits painted during the time of the Apostle Paul. The soil of the island of Malta is comprised of limestone, and the only fresh water comes from wells drilled into the limestone. I mention this because this soil's mineral content is credited with giving the Maltese breed a unique set of requirements for the mineral complex. You will know if this breed is receiving the proper minerals in its diet if its coat remains white and the eye drainage does not stain its face coat. When this breed is receiving the wrong food sources of minerals its coat yellows, and the face coat has a red streaking under the eyes.

Native food supplies for this breed would have been goat, fish, poultry, and highly acidic fruits such as the orange, grape, fig, and avocado. The carbohydrates were from grains of brown rice and barley.

For the Maltese I recommend foods containing salt water fish, poultry, and lamb blended with brown rice, avocado, and wheat. You should avoid feeding a Maltese any sulfate minerals; as well as soy, horse meat, beef, or beet pulp.

145

MANCHESTER TERRIER (Standard & Toy)

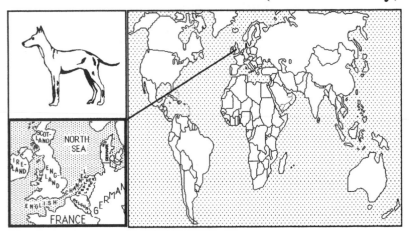

Weight Standards: Standard: m/f - 13 to 22 lbs.; Toy: m/f - under 12 lbs.
Height Standards: Standard: m/f - average 17 inches; Toy: m/f - 12 inches
Coat: both sizes have short and smooth coats in black with tan
Common Ailments: skin rashes, hot spots

The Manchester Terrier developed north of the township of Manchester, England. Originally called the Black and Tan, it was renamed Manchester Terrier in honor of a single breeder who lived in the township of Manchester, England. This one breeder took this terrier from the bloody sport of rat killing and made it a household pet. This breed is very quick and agile, a trait that made it good in the rat pit. For example, one of these dogs killed 100 rats in just 6 minutes and 13 seconds! The Toy Manchester Terrier was developed as a direct descendant of the larger Manchester Terrier by breeders who wanted a smaller variety of this breed. Both sizes of Manchester Terrier are very lean breeds of dog, having very little body fat. This body fat to muscle ratio is a factor in their nutritional requirements. They will do well on a food with a low fat content and can be taken off puppy formulas at an earlier age than many other breeds.

Native food supplies would have included rodents, rabbit, beef, wheat, oats, sugar beet, and ground vegetables.

For both sizes of Manchester Terrier I recommend foods that are low in fats yet high in carbohydrates and fiber. The ingredients I recommend are horse meat with oats, wheat, potato, and beet pulp. However, for these dogs I feel you should avoid feeding any food containing soy, rice, avocado, or yellow corn.

MASTIFF (English & Neapolitan)

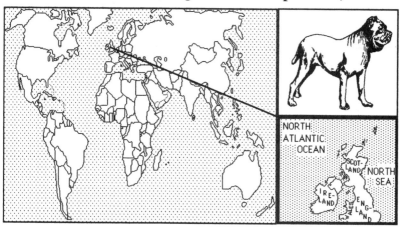

NORTH ATLANTIC OCEAN

SCOT-LAND
NORTH SEA
IRE-LAND
ENG-LAND

Weight Standards: m - average 180 lbs., f - average 170 lbs.
Height Standards: m - over 30 inches, f - over 27.5 inches
Coat: short, dense in texture, colors of fawn, brindle or apricot
Common Ailments: dysplasia, bloat, hot spots

The English Mastiff developed in Great Britain prior to the Roman invasion in 55 B.C.. When the Romans invaded England, they were introduced to an impressively courageous and loyal dog. They brought selective breeding stock back to Italy, which in turn became known as **the Neapolitan Mastiff**. It was used in the Roman Circus to fight lions and bears. There is one story that tells of a single Mastiff fighting a bull elephant, AND WINNING!

Native food supplies for the English Mastiff would have been venison, cattle, wheat, oats, and high carbohydrate sugar beet and potato. The Neapolitan Mastiff was then exposed to more vegetable oils while retaining an exposure to high carbohydrate foods from rye and brown rice sources.

Both the English and Neapolitan variety are nutritionally different from a Tibetan Mastiff, a breed first appearing in Chinese literature around 1121 BC. For both the English and Neapolitan Mastiffs I recommend foods high in carbohydrates and fiber. Their foods should contain beef, wheat, and potato. With the Neapolitan Mastiff you also should include more fatty vegetable oils and some brown rice and avocado. With both you should avoid poultry, lamb, or soy.

MINIATURE PINSCHER

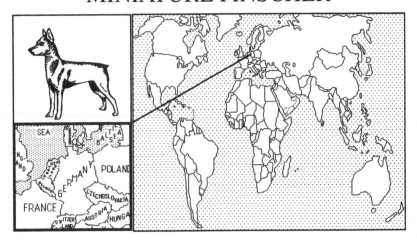

Weight Standards: m/f - 9 lbs.
Height Standards: m/f - 10 to 12.5 inches
Coat: short and smooth textured, in reds or blacks with tan
Common Ailments: hot spots, skin rashes, pigmentation problems, liver and kidney failure

The Miniature Pinscher originated in Germany where its history goes back over many hundreds of years. It was originally a barnyard ratter. It is often called the *Reh Pinscher* in Germany because its appearance is similar to a native species of miniature deer. They are called the Miniature Pinscher in the U.S.A. because their appearance is very similar to a "miniaturized Doberman Pinscher." However, there is no genetic relationship between these two breeds. The Min Pin is wonderful with children and in a family environment. It is also very territorial and possessive. Therefore, it makes an excellent family watch dog. This breed is small and has a sleek appearance, yet it is very "thick boned." This characteristic gives it a different requirement for bone building minerals per pound of body weight than other "small" breeds that are more fragile or "thin boned."

Food supplies from this breed's native environment would have been sugar beet, potato, cabbage, and meats from pork, venison, and rodents.

For the Miniature Pinscher I recommend foods that are a blend of horse meat, beef, wheat, potatoes, yellow corn, and beet pulp. However, you should avoid feeding a food that contains any ocean fish, soy, or rice to this breed.

MINIATURE SCHNAUZER

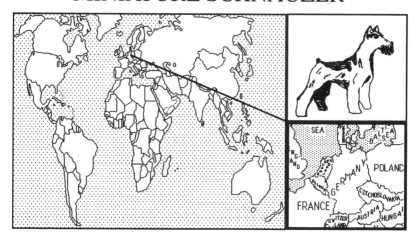

Weight Standards: m/f 14 to 17 lbs.
Height Standards: m/f 12 to 14 inches
Coat: hard & wiry in solid black or salt & pepper or black & silver
Common Ailments: cataracts, kidney problems

The Miniature Schnauzer developed in the farmlands of Germany. It was bred down to its present size by selectively breeding a larger variety of Schnauzer with other smaller German breeds. Which breeds these were has been the topic of many a lively debate amongst Miniature Schnauzer fanciers. Whatever these breeds were, today's Miniature Schnauzer has been in existence since the 15th century. It retained the Schnauzer appearance, with the abundant whiskers and leg furnishings, but developed its own charming personality. This combination of good looks and personality made it one of the most popular miniature breeds.

There are very few breeds of dog that do not shed their coat. The Miniature Schnauzer is one of these rare nonshedders. This feature makes it an ideal pet for people with allergies and also gives it different dietary requirement for hair production than those breeds that are shedders.

Native food supplies found in this breed's homeland would have been beet pulp, wheat, potatoes, cabbage, and meats from rodents and beef cattle. Therefore, for the Miniature Schnauzer I recommend foods that have a blend of horse meat, beef, potato, wheat, and beet pulp. However, I also feel you should avoid feeding a Miniature Schnauzer any soy bean products, avocado, ocean fish, white rice, or brown rice.

NEWFOUNDLAND

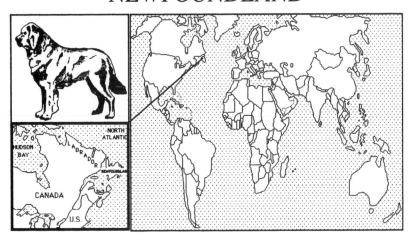

Weight Standards: m - average 150 lbs., f - average 120 lbs.
Height Standards: m - average 28 inches, f - average 26 inches
Coat: double, flat topcoat, black, black & white, bronze, or gray
Common Ailments: dysplasia, skin rashes, hot spots
and pigmentation problems

The Newfoundland originated in the Canadian province of Newfoundland as the companion and co-worker of coastal fisherman. It is only one of six breeds of dog I know of with webbed feet. Nutritional studies of the Newfoundland showed a very high requirement for the fat soluble vitamins A-D-E per kilogram of body weight. However, for this breed these vitamins must come from the proper source. For example, Newfoundland dogs show a very low assimilation rate for vitamin A derived from beta carotene, usually found in carrots or vegetables. Yet vitamin A from fish liver oil or in a palmitate form has a much higher rate of assimilation for the Newfoundland.

Nutrients in the Newfoundland's native environment consisted primarily of cold water white fish such as cod, halibut, and herring. Any exposure to meat would have been from caribou (which has an amino acid profile similar to that of horse meat) and bear (which has an amino acid profile similar to that of pork).

For a Newfoundland I recommend you look for food blends containing fish, pork, poultry, and lamb. The food should have a high fat content. I also advise you to avoid foods composed of beef and soy or any food having a protein content over 30 percent or a high fiber content from oats, beets, or wood pulp.

NORFOLK TERRIER

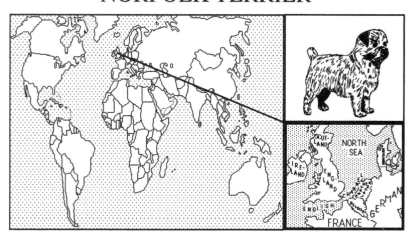

Weight Standards: m/f - 11 to 12 lbs.
Height Standards: m/f - 10 inches
Coat: hard textured and wiry in colors of Wheaton, red, tan or black
Common Ailments: kidney ailments, hot spots and skin rashes

The Norfolk Terrier developed in the area surrounding Norfolk, England. In this farming community of Mideastern England this breed earned its keep as a barnyard ratter. This breed is often confused with the Norwich Terrier because of their similar appearance. The only exterior difference is that the Norfolk has dropped ears and the Norwich has pricked ears. However, these two breeds are different and cross breeding of the two can create problems. Their genetically different nutritional requirements create many of these problems. For example, the minerals the Norfolk Terrier can best assimilate are not the same as the minerals the Norwich can best assimilate.

The native environment for the Norfolk would have provided food supplies from the farmlands. These would have included beef cattle, rodents, beets, wheat, potatoes, and other ground vegetables grown in the region's bogey marshland soil.

For the Norfolk I recommend foods that are a blend of beef and horse meat with carbohydrates from potato, wheat, and beets. I also recommend you avoid feeding a Norfolk any foods that contain ocean fish, avocado, white rice, or soy bean products.

NORWEGIAN ELKHOUND

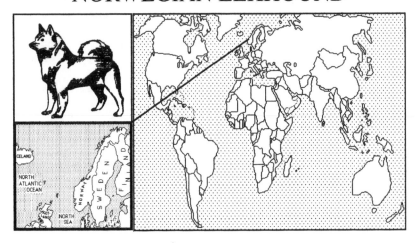

Weight Standards: m - 55 lbs., f - 48 lbs.
Height Standards: m - 20.5 inches, f - 19.5 inches
Coat: short undercoat & longer topcoat, silver gray black tipped
Common Ailments: cysts, dysplasia and PRA

The Norwegian Elkhound is the National Dog of Norway, where it developed prior to the time of the Vikings (800-1000 AD). They became the working companions of the Vikings and were held in high esteem by these people who inhabited this cold and rugged land. Many excavation sites have uncovered the body of a Norwegian Elkhound buried next to its Danish master. They pulled sleds, tended flocks of reindeer, hunted bear and moose, and guarded the family. The Norwegian Elkhound is a compact and well muscled dog that reflects the physical characteristics of a breed developed in a cold rugged country; a country where stamina, rather than flat land speed, was required to survive.

Native food supplies for this breed would have come from the cold and rugged country of Norway. This environment's meat supply came from land animals such as the reindeer, elk, hare, lynx, wolf or bear, all high in their body fat content. The waters of Norway would have produced an abundance of both the salt water and fresh water fish.

For the Norwegian Elkhound I recommend foods that are high in animal fats. The best blends will contain beef and horse meat, with an equal amount of fish. Any carbohydrates in the food can come from potato or wheat, but you should avoid feeding any white rice or soy based food to this breed.

NORWICH TERRIER

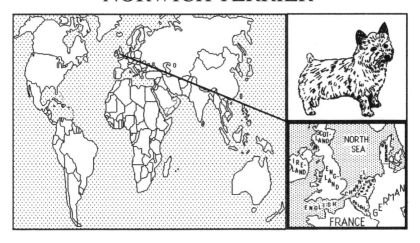

Weight Standards: m/f - 11 to 12 lbs.
Height Standards: m/f - 10 inches
Coat: short and rough in texture, red, wheaton or brindle
Common Ailments: hot spots and skin rashes

The Norwich Terrier developed in Norwich, England, where the Yare and Wensum rivers join. These two rivers then travel the short distance to "Caister on the sea", where the North Sea meets the English Channel. This confluence of rivers close to the coast provided more of a port city environment than the barn yard environment of this breed's Norfolk Terrier ancestors. It also provided this breed with foods uncommon to its inland relatives. The Norwich continued to share many similar food sources with its inland relatives, such as rodents, beef, wheat, oats, potato, and other farmland products. However, it was also exposed to more fish and coastal type foods. I believe the acclamation to these coastal foods, with their different mineral sources, is what gave this breed its requirement for a coastal source of the mineral complex. For example, the Norwich Terrier seems to assimilate calcium from oyster shell better than calcium from bones of animals.

For the Norwich Terrier I recommend foods that are a blend of fish with horse meats, beef, potato, wheat, and oats. The mineral sources that are best for this breed would include sea kelp, oyster shell, and gluconates. The mineral sources to avoid are from animal bone, sulfate or fumerate sources. Other nutrients you should avoid feeding a Norwich are white rice, soy, avocado, and citrus fruits.

NOVA SCOTIA DUCK TOLLING RETRIEVER

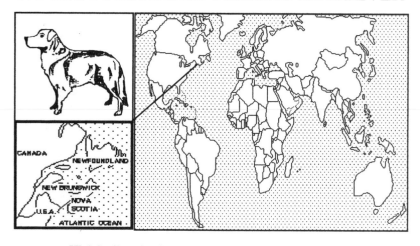

Weight Standards: m - 45 to 51 lbs., f - 37 to 43 lbs.
Height Standards: m - 19 to 20 inches, f - 1 inch less
Coat: medium top coat over dense undercoat, red or orange colors
Common Ailments: hot spots and skin rashes

The Nova Scotia Duck Tolling Retriever developed in Yarmouth County on the Canadian island of Nova Scotia. Yarmouth County is located on the southern tip of Nova Scotia and is directly across a narrow North Atlantic waterway from the eastern coastal states of Maine and Massachusetts, U.S.A. The Canadian Kennel Club gave recognition to this breed in 1945 after it had been bred true for over 200 years. When recognized in 1945 its name was changed from the Little River Duck Dog to its present name. The "*Tolling* " part of its present name comes from a technique it uses when hunting. "*Tolling* " is an unusual technique of onshore antics also used by the wild fox to lure game birds in close for a kill.

Native food supplies for this breed would have included fish of the ocean varieties, domestic poultry, and wild water fowl. There are very few grains native to Nova Scotia and the vegetable crops are limited. Also, records show livestock ranching was not introduced onto the island of Nova Scotia until the 1930's. Since this was long after the development of this breed of dog, their exposure to beef or pork would have been limited.

For the Nova Scotia Duck Tolling Retriever I recommend foods that are a blend of fish, poultry, and potato with small amounts of wheat and oat. I also feel you should avoid feeding this breed any soy products, beef or horse meats, beet pulp, avocado, or rice.

OLD ENGLISH SHEEPDOG

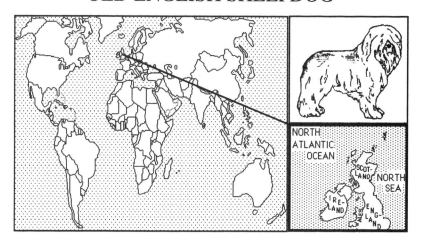

Weight Standards: m - average 90 lbs., f - average 75 lbs.
Height Standards: m - over 22 inches, f - slightly less
Coat: long profuse and shaggy, in white with blue-grey,
blue merle, steel-blue-grey, or black
Common Ailments: hip dysplasia and cataracts

The **Old English Sheepdog** developed in the western and central farmland areas of England. Originally drovers used this breed to herd livestock to market. The English government allowed a tax exemption during the 1700's for dogs the drovers used for their business of herding. The dogs the drovers used for herding were identified by a docked tail. The practice of docking a working dog's tail gave the dog a bobtailed appearance and thus its nickname "the bobtail." This breed is also a good upland retriever. The Old English Sheepdog has a very soft mouth that is good for retrieving a sportsman's kill without further damaging it.

Native food supplies for this breed would have been from the western farmland region of England. They would have consisted of both mutton and a lean form of beef blended with the grain crops of wheat, corn, and oats. This area was also high in its production of beets, potatoes, and leafy green vegetables.

For the Old English Sheepdog I recommend foods that are a blend of lamb, beef, beet pulp, wheat, corn, and potato. However, I feel you should avoid feeding a "bobtail" any ocean fish, poultry by-products, avocado, rice or soy.

OTTER HOUND

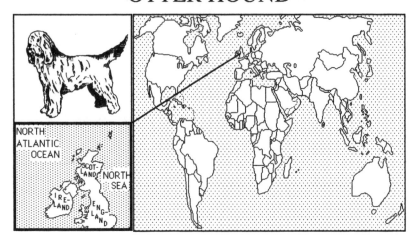

Weight Standards: m - 75 to 115 lbs., f - 65 to 100 lbs.
Height Standards: m - 24 to 27 inches, f - 22 to 26 inches
Coat: shaggy top coat, water resistant, in many colors
Common Ailments: bloat, dysplasia, and hemophilia

The Otter Hound developed in a region of England known for its many streams and excellent fishing. This breed can take a lot of credit for the good fish population in its homeland streams. It was this dog's job to hunt otter that robbed these streams of fish. Records show that the Otter Hound has been bred pure in their native England since the 1300's. Records of this breed also show that its popularity diminished to a point where there were less than 100 Otter Hounds in all of Britain in 1978. At that time Hunt members of the English Kennel Club sponsored a law making this breed a protected species in Britain. In the U.S.A. this breed is growing in popularity and has established itself as a fine hunter of the raccoon, bear, mink, and mountain lion.

Native food supplies for this breed would have been the meats from otter, badger, fish, and rodent. Vegetables were of the type that could grow in the bogey soil of the English region where it developed.

For the Otter Hound I recommend foods that are a blend of fish, poultry, and horse meats combined with potatoes and wheat. The food should have a very high fat content from fish oil or poultry fat. I also recommend that you avoid feeding an Otter Hound any soy products (this includes soy oil coat conditioners), yellow corn, avocado, or white rice.

PAPILLON

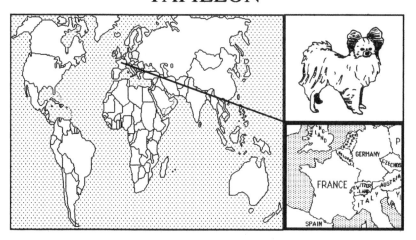

Weight Standards: m/f - average 8 lbs.
Height Standards: m/f - 8 to 11 inches
Coat: long and silky in texture, in any color combined with white
Common Ailments: slipped stifle, fractures easily

The Papillon has been breeding true to its present day standards for the last 700 years in France. There are unsubstantiated rumors that over 700 years ago this breed lived in coastal Italy and came from a dwarf spaniel. The name "Papillon" in French means "*butterfly* " and relates to the breed's ears, which are mobile, erect and fringed with fine hair. There is also a white blaze that runs up the forehead of most of these dogs to further enhance the butterfly appearance. The Papillon also has what some may call a "dainty" appearance, but the breed is not at all what anyone could mistake for dainty. Historically they were a very active ratter and have always been a healthy breed.

Native food supplies for this breed would have been the type found on a 16th century farm in Central France. The meats would have consisted of the farms' rodents, poultry, and mutton with crops of in ground vegetables, wheat, and corn.

For the Papillon I recommend foods that are a blend of poultry, lamb, potato, wheat, and corn. However, I feel you should avoid feeding a Papillon any form of soy products, rice, ocean fish, horse meat, or beef.

PEKINGESE

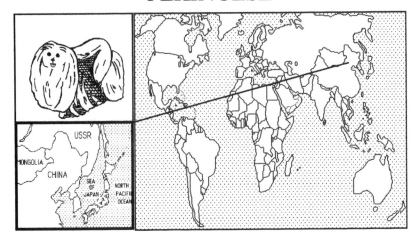

Weight Standards: m/f - under 14 lbs.
Height Standards: m/f - 8 inches
Coat: smooth, long top coat, any color but liver and white
Common Ailments: eye lacerations, respiratory & spinal problems

The Pekingese developed within the Summer Imperial Palace in Peking, China, during the 8th century. Ownership of this dog was restricted to the members of the Chinese Imperial Court. The Pekinese was considered to be a good luck charm for their owners. They were called by three names in their early years: Lion Dog (because of their appearance), Sun Dog, and Sleeve Dog (because they could be carried about in sleeves). Due to their confinement within the Imperial Palace, they were unknown to the outside world until the British invasion of the Palace in 1860. When the British troops invaded the Palace they found five of these small dogs guarding the body of their mistress, an imperial princess. These five were captured by the invading troops, taken to England, and are the forefathers of the Pekingese found in this country today.

Native food supplies for this breed would have been those used in the kitchens of the Imperial Palace in Peking, China, and would have been foods of the Mandarin variety. They would have consisted of meats from fish, pork, and poultry with greens, beets, rice, and soy products.

For the Pekingese of today I recommend foods that are a blend of poultry, rice, yellow corn, beet, and soy. However, I feel you should avoid feeding a Pekingese any white potatoes, avocado, oats, beef, or horse meat.

PEMBROKE WELSH CORGI

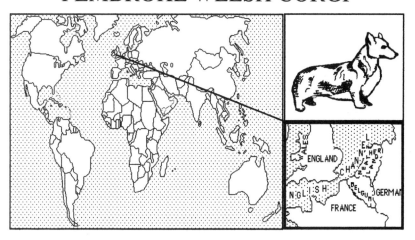

Weight Standards: m - 30 lbs. or less, f - 28 lbs. or less
Height Standards: m/f - 10 to 12 inches
Coat: short & rough textured, red, red & black, or sable & white
Common Ailments: hot spots, kidney and liver disorders

The **Pembroke Welsh Corgi** developed in the area of Pembrokeshire, Wales. This area is on the southernmost part of Wales where St. Gowans Head protrudes into the Bristol Channel, close to the North Sea. This southern part of Wales has always been known for its mines and seaports, but it has never been good for growing any crops or farming. The first records we have of this single breed of dog are dated prior to 1100 A. D.. The records provide evidence that this breed has not changed since that time.

Native food supplies for the Pembroke Welsh Corgi breed came from the Southern Coastal Region of Wales and, therefore, were very high in their mineral content. Since the mineral concentrations were high in this breed's native dietary intake, today's Pembroke Welsh Corgi's mineral requirement remains very high when compared to other breeds. Also, the Pembroke Welsh Corgi's dietary minerals of Calcium, Phosphorus, and Iodine should come from a coastal source.

For the Pembroke Welsh Corgi I recommend foods that are a blend of fish, lamb, poultry, potato, beets, carrots, and barley. However, I feel you should avoid feeding this breed any horse meat, beef, soy, citrus fruits, or avocado.

PHARAOH HOUND

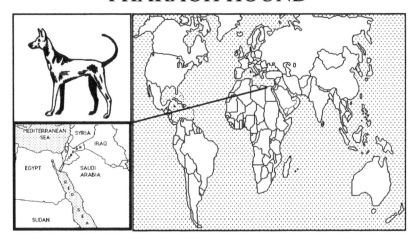

Weight Standards: m/f - average 45 to 55 lbs.
Height Standards: m - 23 to 24 inches, f - 21 to 23 inches
Coat: single, red, copper brown or tan, light flesh color nose
Common Ailments: pigmentation, kidney and liver problems

The Pharaoh Hound originated in the deserts of Egypt where it was revered by King Tutankhamen over 3000 years ago. It was then taken to the Mediterranean Islands of Gazo and Malta by Phoenician traders over 2000 years ago. It is from the stock bred true on these Mediterranean Islands for the last 2000 years that the world has today's Pharaoh Hounds. They were originally brought to the islands to control the rabbit populations and were extremely successful at their job. In appreciation for their work, they were declared the National Dog of Malta. This breed has many unique characteristics. Two of the most interesting physical characteristics are: they have an absence of "doggie odor" when wet, and they "blush" when excited.

Native food supplies for this breed would have been desert gazelle, partridge, goat, rabbit, and fish with grains of brown rice and barley. There were also fruits like the olive and avocado. The mineral content of the drinking waters from their Mediterranean islands is also unique. The islands are comprised of limestone and all drinking water comes from wells drilled into this rock.

For a Pharaoh Hound I recommend foods that use ocean fish, poultry, lamb, avocado, wheat, and corn. However, I feel you should avoid feeding a Pharaoh Hound any white rice, beef or horse meats, soy, beet pulp, or potato.

POINTER

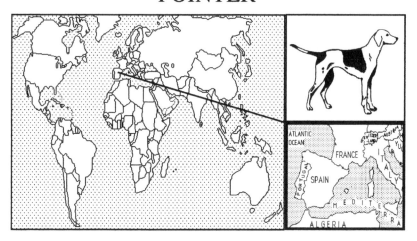

Weight Standards: m - 55 to 75 lbs., f - 45 to 65 lbs.
Height Standards: m - 25 to 28 inches, f - 23 to 26 inches
Coat: short and dense in liver, lemon, black or orange with white
Common Ailments: hip dysplasia, PRA, and cysts

The Pointer is one breed of dog named for the work it does instead of its area of origin. The work at which it has always excelled is the pointing out of upland feathered game. This breed developed in Spain prior to the mid 1600's and was later refined into the Pointer of today by Major Arkwright in Great Britain. The Major selectively bred his kennel of Pointers with breeds like the Setter, Greyhound, and English Foxhound to develop a dog that was faster, had more stamina, and better scenting power than the dogs he first received from European hunting kennels. The Pointers brought to this country from Great Britain in 1880 set the breed standards for all of today's Pointers.

Native food supplies found in the area of Spain where the first Pointer originated consisted of goat, fish, pork, poultry (woodcock, chukker, etc.), brown rice, and citrus fruits. During its short stay in England (about 200 years) it was exposed to more cattle and potato types of vegetables. This temporary change in available nutrients did not seem to change the long term dietary requirements of the Pointer. The Pointer still does better on brown rice than on English potatoes.

For the Pointer I recommend foods that use a blend of brown rice, avocado, poultry, and fish. I also feel you should avoid feeding any soy, beet pulp, beef and horse meat or their by-products to this breed.

161

POMERANIAN

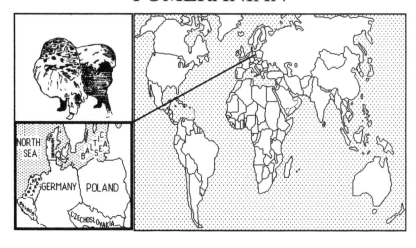

Weight Standards: m/f - 3 to 7 lbs.
Height Standards: m/f - 6 inches
Coat: Dense stand-out coat, any color
Common Ailments: slipped stifle

The Pomeranian is a direct descendent of a thirty pound British herding dog transported to an area of North Central Europe during the Middle Ages. There this thirty pound dog was bred with a smaller breed from Iceland, known as a "Spits dog", and the breed we now know as the Pomeranian developed. The three pound dog that developed in this area is now the smallest member of the Spits family of dogs. It was for the Prussian province of Pomerania, where this cross breeding took place, that the resulting toy sized herding/Spits dog was named.

Pomerania is in an area that is now part of Eastern Germany and Northwestern Poland. This historic region stretches along the Baltic Sea from a line west of Stralsund to the Vistula River in Poland. Principal crops of the Pomerania area included rye, oats, sugar beets, barley, and wheat. The meats of this area included beef cattle and pork as well as fish from both the Baltic Sea and many fresh water rivers. These food sources gave the Pomeranian its basic nutritional requirements.

For this breed I recommend a food that is a blend of fish, beef, horse meat, rye wheat, and beet pulp. I also recommend that you do not feed a Pomeranian foods that include poultry, lamb, rice, or soy.

POODLE (Miniature)

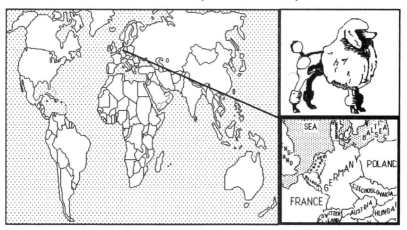

Weight Standards: m/f - 15 to 17 lbs.
Height Standards: m/f - 11 to 15 inches
Coat: Long, dense & harsh textured, curly when clipped, any color
Common Ailments: PRA, eye and ear infections

The Miniature Poodle developed in Northern Germany as a direct descendant of the Standard Poodle. It was selectively bred to its present size in its native Germany during the late 1500's and early 1600's. It has been reported that the Miniature Poodle has the keenest scenting ability of all Poodles, which makes it the best Poodle for finding a subterranean fungus called the *truffle*. Yet the Miniature is very much a water dog and only one of six dogs known to have webbed feet for swimming. The fact that they are first and foremost a water dog also brought about the "Poodle Cut", which was originally designed to lighten the dog's coat while swimming. This cut provides protective cover for the dog's joints and vital organs while in cold water. A multi-purpose dog, today it is the most popular of the Poodle breeds world-wide.

Native food supplies for this breed would have been from the areas of the Black Forest to the Baltic Sea in Northern Germany. These would have consisted of fish, poultry, pork, venison, potato, cabbage, wheat, and corn.

For the Miniature Poodle I recommend foods that are a blend of poultry, fish, wheat, oats, and corn. However, I also feel you should avoid feeding any beef, horse meat, soy, beet pulp, or avocado to a Miniature Poodle.

POODLE (Standard)

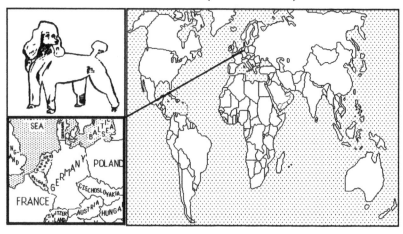

Weight Standards: m/f - 45 to 65 lbs.
Height Standards: m - 24 to 26 inches, f - 22 to 24 inches
Coat: Long, dense, harsh coat, curly when clipped, any color
Common Ailments: PRA, eye & ear infections, bloat & dysplasia

The Standard Poodle originated in Northern Germany as a water fowl retriever. The breed name, which is shared by all sizes of "Poodle", comes from the German word *puddeln* ("to splash in the water"). The Standard has the longest history of all Poodles and the family tree for both the Miniature and Toy can be traced back to the Standard.

The American Kennel Club recognizes the Standard as one part of the Poodles, with the only difference being size amongst the toy, miniature, and the Standard. Nutritionally, however, most Poodle breeders will tell you there are many differences per pound of body weight between the Standard Poodle and its relatives. The Standard Poodle requires protein with high amounts of the amino acid Phenylalanine. The Standard also requires substantial amounts of the mineral complex. When these are lacking in the Standard's diet, the most noticeable change usually occurs in the pigmentation of the skin, gums, and coat. When these nutrients are very low, or from the wrong source, the coat can turn orange in color and lose its luster, and the gums can become very loose around the teeth.

The nutrients of the Northern German area where the Standard Poodle originated consisted of grains like wheat and corn and meat sources like fowl, fish, and pork. Therefore, I recommend foods with a blend of wheat, corn, fish, and poultry for the Standard Poodle. I also suggest that you avoid blends with soy, horse meat, beef by-products, or beet pulp for the Standard.

POODLE (Toy)

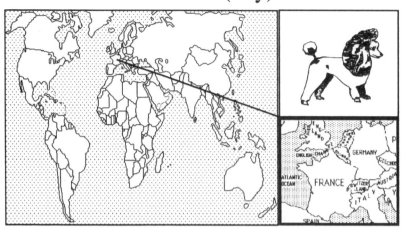

Weight Standards: m/f - 6 lbs.
Height Standards: m/f - 10 inches or under
Coat: Long, dense, harsh coat, curly when clipped; any color
Common Ailments: slipped stifle, PRA, runny eyes, ear infections

The Toy Poodle was a favorite of the French Monarch Louis XVI and developed in France. This exposed it to nutrients that were very different from the native nutrients fed to its German forefathers; the Standard and Miniature Poodles.

When researching this breed's dietary requirements, I discovered some interesting differences. The molecular form of calcium found in beef bone meal can cause the Toy Poodle dietary distress, but the molecular form of calcium found in oyster shells is assimilated well by the Toy Poodle. Also the fat soluble Vitamins A and D should be from palmitate or fish liver, and you should avoid vegetable sources such as beta carotene. You can judge a Toy Poodle's assimilation of these nutrients by observing the condition of the animal's skin and mouth tissue (please see chapter on *A Home Health Check for Symptoms of Nutritional Problems*).

Nutritionally, there are many differences per pound of body weight between the Toy Poodle and its larger relatives. The native foods of Central France where the Toy Poodle developed were much higher in carbohydrates than the foods of Northern Germany where their larger relatives developed. Therefore, I suggest a blend of horse meat with flax, wheat, oats, beets, and corn for the Toy. I also recommend that you do not feed this breed any food containing rice, soy, or avocado.

PORTUGUESE WATER DOG

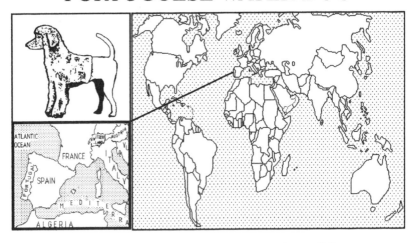

Weight Standards: m - 42 to 60 lbs., f - 35 to 50 lbs.
Height Standards: m - 20 to 23 inches, f - 17 to 21 inches
Coat: profuse, in black, brown solid or combined with white
Common Ailments: liver & kidney disorders, skin rashes, hot spots

The Portuguese Water Dog developed *on the water* off the coast of Portugal. They spent most of their life on the water as a working member of the fishing crew on Portuguese vessels. It was their job to be a ship to ship or ship to shore courier, dive for lost tackle, or drive schools of fish into the nets. These duties required a very special breed of dog. They had to have the stamina to swim for hours and the intelligence to be trained to do what most people would agree is very unusual work for a dog! Physically they are also very special when compared to many land breeds. They never shed their coat, their very lean body can store large energy reserves, and they have webbed feet for swimming. And yes, their special physical characteristics have also given them special dietary needs.

Native food supplies for this breed would have been the same as any crew member on board an 8th century Portuguese fishing vessel and very different from a land animal's diet. They would have subsisted on a diet of fish blended with rice and nuts cooked in olive oil. Fruits were citrus fruits or dried figs.

The Portuguese Water Dog is one of the breeds that needs to have a food made for its unique requirements. I recommend that you feed them their protein, vitamins and minerals from coastal or ocean sources and avoid products like beets, potatoes, soy, beef, or horse meat.

PUG

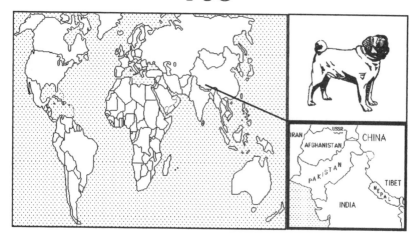

Weight Standards: m/f - 14 to 18 lbs.
Height Standards: m/f - 13 inches
Coat: Short, glossy coat, black or fawn
Common Ailments: eye lacerations, respiratory problems,
heat prostration

The Pug originated in the lowlands of Tibet, a very mountainous environment. The specific area the Pug can call home has an average elevation of 16,000 feet. This elevation affected the climate, natural vegetation, and wildlife. The Pug was no exception. The only meat sources available for the Pug to eat would have been native species of rodent, goat, deer, boar, horse, or Yak. Principal grain sources from this area would have included barley, rye, and mountain corn. Due to the mountain climate of Tibet, meat sources have a high fat content and the requirement of a high fat-to-protein ratio remains with this breed.

There are no commercial all-breed dog foods providing the food sources upon which Pugs developed, and most food ingredients don't come close to the amino acid profiles of the breed's original nutrient sources.

This breed has demonstrated it can do well on a base diet that is high in animal fats from beef and horse meat. The protein content of the food should be kept very low. Any grains in the food should come from barley, wheat and rice. I also suggest that you avoid feeding a Pug any foods containing lamb, poultry, ocean fish, avocado, or yellow corn.

PULI

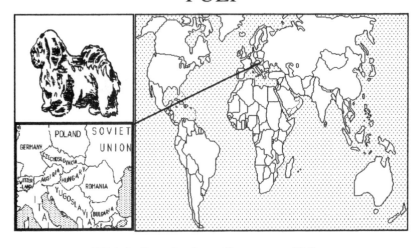

Weight Standards: m/f - average 30 lbs.
Height Standards: m - 17 to 19 inches, f - 16 to 18 inches
Coat: double, naturally corded long top coat, black, gray or white
Common Ailments: dysplasia, skin ailments, pigmentation

The Puli of today developed over the last 1000 years in Hungary. Before that time they were the working companions of the Magyars of Central Asia. They are the most popular breed of dog in Hungary today and have earned their popularity by being both hard workers and pleasant companions. They are very quick and agile, and the work that they do best is the herding of cattle and sheep.

The region of Hungary that the Puli has lived in for the last 1000 years is known as the food basket of Europe. It grows many different crops and provides large amounts of meat for the rest of the European continent. Native food supplies for this breed would have been very diverse. They would have included crops such as wheat, barley, rye, flax, oats, sugar beet, potato, and greens. Meats included beef, lamb, poultry, and pork. This exposure to such a wide range of food sources has provided the Puli with an ability to use many commercial dog food formulas today.

For the Puli I recommend foods that contain horse meat, beef, poultry, barley, oats, wheat, and sugar beet. The food should have a high fiber and protein content of about 24% to 26% but a very low fat content. I also feel that you should avoid feeding a Puli any soy products (including coat conditioners), avocado, white rice, or citrus products.

RHODESIAN RIDGEBACK

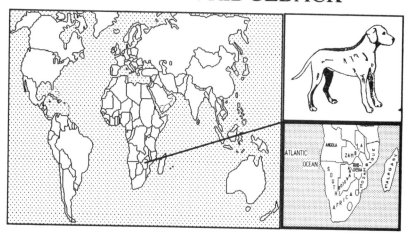

Weight Standards: m - 75 lbs., f - 65 lbs.
Height Standards: m - 25 to 27 inches, f - 24 to 26 inches
Coat: a short single and sleek coat, light to dark Wheaton in color
Common Ailments: Dermoid sinus, hot spots, pigmentation

The Rhodesian Ridgeback developed prior to the 16th century in Southern Africa. As one of the native South African ridged dogs, they were family pets and guard dogs. They are extremely protective of small children and protected the villagers' children from wild animals, including the Lion. Because they could hold a Lion at bay, big game hunters used this breed for commercial reasons. These hunters would have the dog hold a Lion at bay in order for their clients to take the time to make a good shot. Cornelius van Rooyen, a big game hunter from Rhodesia, is credited with making the breed known to the rest of the world. This breed is now named the Rhodesian Ridgeback because of where this one man hunted and because of a ridge of hair on the dog's back, which runs in the opposite direction to the rest of the coat.

Native food supplies for this breed would have been from the African scrub. These consisted of lion, elephant, gazelle, zebra, wilder-beast, goat, poultry, rabbit, other small game animals, ground nuts (like a peanut), brown rice, and wheat.

For the Rhodesian Ridgeback I recommend foods that are a blend of horse meat, poultry, lamb, wheat, avocado, and brown rice. I also suggest that you avoid feeding any white rice, beef, white potato, or soy (including any soy oil coat conditioners) to this breed.

ROTTWEILER

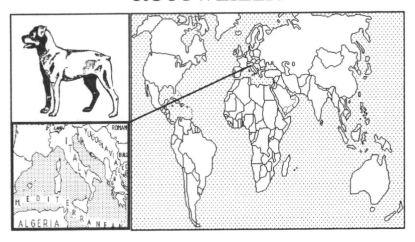

Weight Standards: m - average 115 lbs., f - average 100 lbs.
Height Standards: m - 23 3/4 to 27 inches, f - 21 3/4 to 25 3/4 inches
Coat: Short, flat coat, black with mahogany
Common Ailments: hip dysplasia

The Rottweiler originated in Italy. It was brought to Southern Germany by Hannible as a guard dog and pack animal for his troops. It completed its development into the dog we know today in the township of Rotteil, Germany, which is a small hamlet in the foothills of the German Alps. It is from this small hamlet that this breed received its current name.

Nutritionally the Rottweiler is a breed that should be treated as a puppy for 18 to 24 months, even though they usually reach their full adult size in 10 to 12 months. The Rottweiler's skeletal systems and muscle structure are both slow to develop. A 12-month-old dog may appear to be fully grown, but it is still a puppy in terms of its nutritional needs. When this breed is fed an adult dog food too early, there is a higher chance for developing dysplasia or other bone and muscle problems. When kept on the puppy formulas and schedules until they become adults (nutritionally) they will have fewer problems later.

The nutrients of its native Italy included high carbohydrate grain products. The nutrients found in the mountains of Southern Germany were lamb, poultry, goat, and cheeses. Note: all of these nutrients are high in their fat content.

I have found that the ideal base diet for the Rottweiler would consist of a blend of lamb, poultry, dairy products, and wheat. Foods for this breed to avoid would include fish, horse meat, beef, corn, soy, or white rice.

SAINT BERNARD

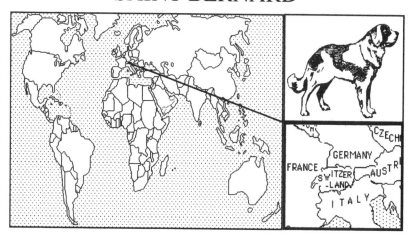

Weight Standards: m - around 165 lbs., f - around 145 lbs.
Height Standards: m - over 27 1/2 inches, f - over 25 1/2 inches
Coat: two varieties; short and long, in red and white with black
Common Ailments: hip dysplasia, bloat, tumors, skin rashes

The Saint Bernard was originally from the foothills of the Alps and a farmer's working companion. They were taken from their native environment to a Hospice in the Swiss Alps in 1660. It was here they performed the rescue work that made them famous. Monks from the *Hospice du Grand St. Bernard* identified some special characteristics in this breed that they felt made them very suitable to do rescue work in the mountains around the Hospice. These special characteristics were stamina, both a heavy double coat and a heavy fat layer to provide thermal protection from prolonged exposure in the snow, and an extraordinary sense of smell and hearing. Some of these same physical characteristics determine their unique nutritional requirements.

Native food supplies for this breed would have been mutton, goat, dairy products, wheat, and low ground vegetables. The vegetables were the type that could grow in the short growing season found in the foothills of the Swiss Alps.

For the Saint Bernard of today I recommend foods of lamb with wheat and potato. However, I also feel that you should avoid feeding any food made with white rice, soy, yellow corn, avocado, horse meat or beef to this breed.

171

SALUKI

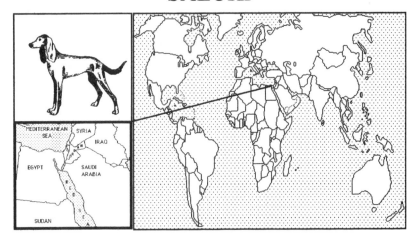

Weight Standards: m/f - 50 to 60 lbs.
Height Standards: m/f - 23-28 inches
Coat: single, silky in texture, flat, in any color but solid black
Common Ailments: circulatory problems, skin rashes and hot spots

The Saluki developed in Ancient Mesopotamia prior to the invasion of the Persian Empire by Alexander the Great (356-323 B.C.). Moslems inhabiting this area declared this breed sacred. It was the only animal allowed to sleep on the carpet of a Sheikh's tent. As a favorite of the sheiks, they were never sold but given as gifts. Because of this they became known as a breed of royalty.

Mesopotamia (today's Egypt) is a hot and humid area. Therefore, unlike many breeds that developed thermal layers of fat to protect them from a cold environment, the Saluki is a breed with very little body fat. This physical characteristic is just one reason this breed has unique nutritional requirements.

Foods found in their native environment would have included camel, goat, rabbit, poultry, other small desert game animals, brown rice, wheat, oils (olive), and citrus fruits. Food supplies that developed this breed were influenced by both the environment and the religious beliefs of their Moslem owners. The Moslem faith prohibits the consumption of beef in any form. Therefore, this breed would not have been exposed to this type of meat.

For the Saluki I recommend foods that contain poultry, brown rice, wheat, and avocado. I also recommend that you avoid feeding any soy, white rice, beef, or horse meat to this breed.

172

SAMOYED

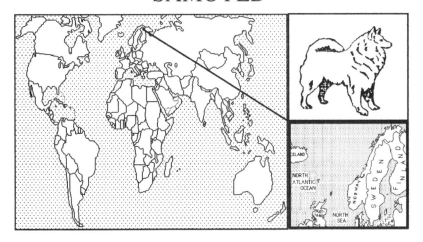

Weight Standards: m - 55 to 75 lbs., f - 40 to 55 lbs.
Height Standards: m - 21 to 23 1/2 inches, f -19 to 21 inches
Coat: Full, long top coat, white, biscuit
Common Ailments: hip dysplasia

The Samoyed originated in the area of the world know by modern man as Finland. They are named after the Samoyedes, nomadic tribesmen who domesticated and trained these dogs. These dogs were taught to guard and drive the tribe's reindeer and caribou herds in their Northern Arctic circle homeland. Samoyedes used this breed as draft and sled dogs and household companions. As one of the larger breeds of the Spitz family of dogs, they have changed little over the last 2000 years. In fact this breed of dog has lain claim to being the most nearly akin to the primitive dog. I know of no other breed that disputes this claim.

Principal nutrients of their native area have also changed very little in the past 2000 years. These nutrients consist of reindeer, fish, whale, and caribou meat with potatoes and fodder beets. Any grain crops would include a form of oats, wheat, and barley.

For the Samoyed I recommend dog foods that are a blend of horse meat, poultry, and fish with wheat and potatoes. To the food I suggest you include about 1 teaspoon of Tuna fish for each adult feeding per day. The tuna should be the type canned in water. DO NOT USE TUNA CANNED IN SOY OIL! I also recommend that you avoid feeding the Samoyed any foods that contain avocado, lamb, soy, or yellow corn.

SCHIPPERKE

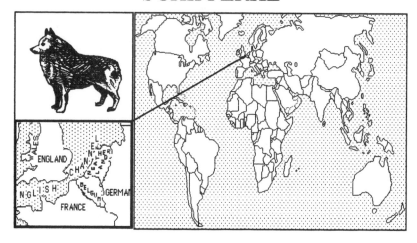

Weight Standards: m/f - 18 lbs. or under
Height Standards: m/f - 12 to 23 inches
Coat: Short dense under coat, stand-out top coat, black in color
Common Ailments: hot spots and skin rashes

The Schipperke developed in Flanders before the 12th century. This small lowland country became part of Belgium in 1830. The Schipperke was a barge dog and companion to the boatmen who worked the channels of this lowland country for centuries. The name Schipperke in Flemish means "little boatman." This breed also served as a ratter and carriage dog in the towns along the channels.

A very active breed of dog, it burns calories at an exceptionally high rate on a per pound basis when compared with many lethargic breeds. Today's Schipperke is also one of the few breeds that lives an average of 15 to 16 years of age. Such longevity is a very rare occurrence within the canine family today. I attribute this longevity to this breed's efficient utilization of food and to its high activity level, which keeps it in good shape.

Native food supplies for this breed would have consisted of both ocean and fresh water fish, dairy cattle, grains from the barges, beets, and other low ground type vegetables.

For the Schipperke I recommend foods that contain an equal amount of beef blended with fish. The food also should contain wheat, oats yellow corn, and beets. I also feel you should avoid feeding a Schipperke any soy, avocado, white rice, lamb, or citrus products.

SCOTTISH DEERHOUND

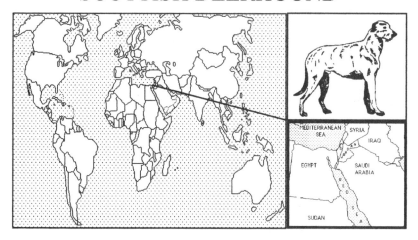

Weight Standards: m - 85 to 110 lbs., f - 75 to 95 lbs.
Height Standards: m - over 30 inches, f - over 28 inches
Coat: short, harsh and ragged in various shades of gray
Common Ailments: bloat and dysplasia

The Scottish Deerhound is a direct descendant of an Egyptian desert sight hound. It was brought to Scotland by Phoenician traders prior to 1000 B.C.. In the Northern Highlands of Scotland their human companions used this breed to run down and kill the native species of deer. This species of deer can stand about six feet at the shoulder and has an average weight of 250 lbs. Therefore, this breed needed to be very fleet and very strong to do the job required. It has retained those breed specific physical attributes to this day. However, its waterproof and shaggy coat may have developed during its time in the Northern Highlands.

Native food supplies from the Scottish Highlands included the venison from the Scottish deer, poultry, wheat, flax, corn, and potatoes. Foods from their Egyptian homeland would have included desert game animals, brown rice, citrus fruits, lamb and poultry.

For the Scottish Deerhound I recommend foods that are very high in carbohydrates. These foods should use a blend of lamb, poultry, potatoes, wheat and corn. I also recommend that you should avoid feeding a Scottish Deerhound any beef, horse meat, soy, white rice, or beet pulp.

175

SCOTTISH TERRIER

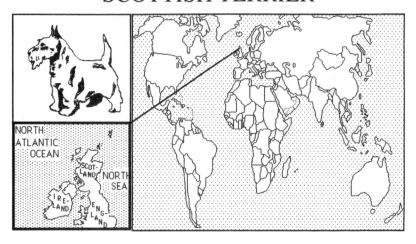

Weight Standards: m - 19 to 22 lbs., f - 18 to 21 lbs.
Height Standards: m/f - about 10 inches
Coat: double with long topcoat (on sides), wiry in texture,
black, wheaton or shades of brindle
Common Ailments: skin ailments, hot spots, Scottie cramp

The Scottish Terrier is the oldest pure highland terrier breed of dog. Records show they have not changed since the 1500's. They originally hunted the fox living in rocky boroughs of the Scottish Highlands. They were named for both their area of development as well as their Terrier heritage. First introduced into the dog show world in the early 1800's, they were shown as the "Hard - Haired Scotch Terrier". They were called this because of a rough and wiry topcoat. This wiry topcoat seems to be prevalent among all sizes of breeds that developed in the highlands of Scotland. This breed has a gait that is a peculiarity in itself, unlike any other breed of dog from Scotland or anywhere else. Many Scottie breeders claim this gait is a true indicator of the breed's unique personality.

Native food supplies for this breed would have included mutton, poultry, and a form of dairy cattle now found in the Aberdeen Scotland area only. Predominant vegetable and grain crops were potatoes, corn, and wheat.

For the Scottie I recommend foods that are high in their carbohydrates and low in their protein percentages. These foods should have a blend of poultry, mutton, wheat, corn, and potatoes. I also feel that you should avoid feeding a Scottish Terrier any horse meat, soy products, beet pulp, white rice, or avocado.

SEALYHAM TERRIER

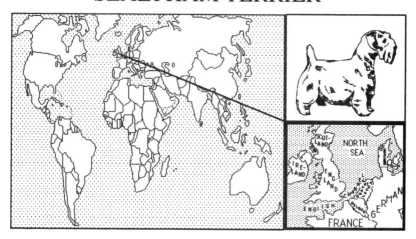

Weight Standards: m/f - 23 to 24 lbs.
Height Standards: m/f - average 10.5 inches
Coat: A hard long top coat in solid white
Common Ailments: spinal disc problems, skin rashes and hot spots

The Sealyham Terrier is a new breed of dog. It developed on the Sealyham Estates of Captain John Edwards in Great Britain during the mid to late 1800's. Captain Edwards developed this breed by blending many other breeds of dog commonly found in the area of his Sealyham Estate. The breeds that are the forefathers of the Sealyham Terrier are the Bull Terrier, Corgi, Dandie Dinmont Terrier, Flanders Basset, Fox Terrier, Old English Terrier and West Highland Terrier. Captain Edward's goal was to develop a breed of terrier that was fearless and tough, fast enough to work with Otter Hounds as a hunt terrier, and agile enough to slip down a badger hole in pursuit of quarry.

To trace the native food supplies for this breed we would have to consider all the breeds that went into the development of the Sealyham Terrier. However, this is very easy since they were all from the same area and were thus exposed to the same basic dietary environment. This environment would have provided these breeds with meats from their hunting, (the fox, otter, and badger), and with domesticated poultry and mutton. The vegetable crops were those that could grow in this area's rocky soil, such as cabbage, potatoes, wheat, and yellow corn.

For the Sealyham Terrier I recommend foods that are a blend of horse meat, mutton, poultry, corn, wheat, and potatoes. However, I feel you should avoid feeding this breed any white rice, soy, avocado, or ocean fish.

SHETLAND SHEEPDOG

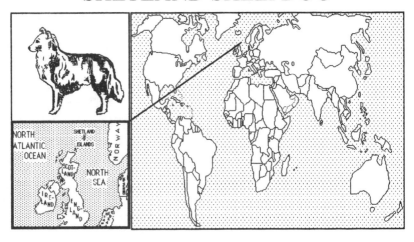

Weight Standards: m/f - average 18 lbs.
Height Standards: m/f - 13 to 16 inches
Coat: Long, straight, dense coat, Collie colors
Common Ailments: Collie Eye and epilepsy

The Shetland Sheepdog originated on the Shetland Islands off the coast of Scotland. The dog's job was to control small flocks of sheep and to watch over toddlers at play. To this day, Shelties display a strong sense of boundary, a legacy from their earlier working days. The calcium source that the Sheltie best assimilates is also traced to its native environment. Breeders have found that calcium from animal bone sources can cause kidney stones in this breed. Yet calcium from a coastal ocean environment, like that found in oyster shells, is easily and completely assimilated. Also the unusual type of iodine contained in the soil on the Shetland Islands is credited with altering the thyroxine produced by the thyroid gland of the Sheltie's forefathers. Since thyroxine stimulates the pituitary gland and thus determines body size, the environmental effect created the "Small Collie" or Sheltie of today.

Nutrients native to the Shetland Islands were all influenced by the environment's unique mineral balance. These included pork, goat, lamb, fish, and vegetables, such as potato, carrots, and cabbage.

I recommend a blend of lamb, fish, potato, and barley for today's Shetland Sheepdog. Nutrients this breed should avoid are avocado, beef, soy, yellow corn, or beet meal.

SHIBA INU

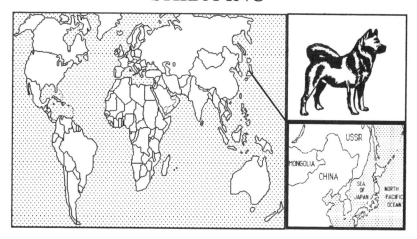

Weight Standards: m/f - 45 to 55 lbs.
Height Standards: m/f - 14 to 16 inches
Coat: double, topcoat hard textured, a variety of colors; red-peppered, black-peppered, solid black, black-brown, brindle or white
Common Ailments: pigmentation problems, skin rashes, hot spots

The Shiba Inu developed in Central Japan in the prefectures of Gifu, Nagano, and Toyama. This breed resembles a small Akita, which also developed in the same region. The Shiba Inu's name translates to "little dog." Therefore, it has been theorized that development of this breed came about through selective breeding of Akitas. However, I have found no records confirming this theory; and for all we know, the Akita could have developed from selective breeding of Shiba Inus. In Japan the Shiba Inu hunted small game, such as the squirrels, birds, and hare that lived in the foothills. Its quickness and legendary intelligence have been great assets.

The native food supplies for this breed would have included meat from the small game they hunted. This meat was blended with rice, a tuber type of root much like our sweet potato, green vegetables, and cabbage.

For the Shiba Inu I recommend foods that are a blend of poultry, lamb, white fish, and rice. I also recommend that you avoid feeding a Shiba Inu any yellow corn, white potato, beet pulp, beef, horse meat, avocado, or citrus product.

179

SHIH TZU

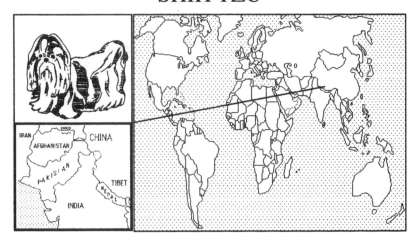

Weight Standards: m/f - 12 to 15 lbs.
Height Standards: m/f - 9 to 10 inches
Coat: Long, dense, slightly wavy coat, all colors
Common Ailments: eye, ear, and respiratory problems

The Shih Tzu, the "lion dog", originated in Tibet. The forefathers of today's Shih Tzu were presented as a tribute gift of state to the Chinese emperor over 2000 years ago. At that time the emperor resided in an area now known as Peking. The exports of this breed to the rest of the world have come from this area of China. Therefore most people have forgotten its Tibetan origins and have given the people of Peking credit for both naming and developing this breed.

Today's Shih Tzu requires a high animal and poultry fat diet at all stages of its life cycle. This is due to the original dietary sources for the Shih Tzu (both Tibet and Peking, China) being high in their fat-to-protein ratios. The Shih Tzu does not store this fat but converts it into energy within hours. For this reason it is best to feed this breed small quantities of foods with a high fat to protein ratio at frequent intervals daily.

In its development the Shih Tzu enjoyed a diet consisting of poultry, pork, barley, rice, soy, and the castles' rodents. A blend of these nutrients would be best for the Shih Tzu today. I recommend a blend of poultry, soy, rice, and wheat. Conversely, I believe the least desirable blend for the Shih Tzu would consist of beef, yellow corn, or oats.

SIBERIAN HUSKY

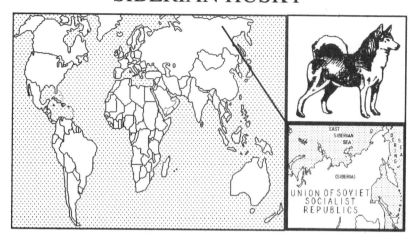

Weight Standards: m - 45 to 60 lbs., f - 35 to 50 lbs.
Height Standards: m - 21 to 23 1/2 inches, f - 20 to 22 inches
Coat: Short, dense coat, all colors
Common Ailments: hip dysplasia, PRA, cataracts

The Siberian Husky originated in the steppes area of Siberia. This breed gained international recognition in 1925 when a dog sled team comprised of Sibes delivered diphtheria serum to Nome, Alaska, and an epidemic was diverted. This was done despite extremely adverse weather conditions and after many other dog teams comprised of other breeds had tried but failed. A statue of the lead dog from that team, *Balto*, now stands in Central Park, New York.

When compared to other breeds, the Siberian Husky's need for carbohydrates per kilogram of body weight is very low. Yet, the breed has a high requirement for fatty acids. The breed's fatty acids must come from sources that contain the proper balance of linolenic, linoleic, and oleic acids. These three fatty acids must be balanced correctly for the Siberian Husky to convert them to the arachidonic acid its body makes. Also, the Siberian stands out nutritionally as the only breed of dog that I know of that has never had a reported case of salmon poisoning.

The native diet of the Sibe consisted of salmon, fresh water fish, and animals like otter and mink that are very high in their fat content. For this breed I recommend food based on a blend of fish and poultry. These sources would provide the best sources of both fats and protein for a Siberian Husky. I also suggest you avoid dog foods based on beef, horse meat, soy, avocado, yellow corn, or beet pulp.

SILKY TERRIER

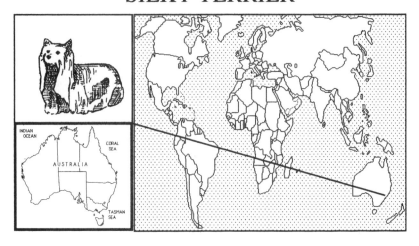

Weight Standards: m/f - 8 to 10 lbs.
Height Standards: m/f - 9 to 10 inches
Coat: Long, straight, silky coat, blue-and-tan
Common Ailments: Reportedly a hardy breed with few ailments

The Silky Terrier, a relatively new breed, originated in the township of Sydney, Australia, in the late 1800's. It developed as the result of a cross breeding program between the Australian Terrier and the Yorkshire Terrier. The Silky was developed for the sole purpose of being an attractive household pet. This breed is very easy going for a Terrier and thrives on a lot of companionship.

Reportedly, table scraps that contain salts or beef fats can cause this breed nutritional problems. Also the Silky Terrier has very high requirements (based on Kilogram of body weight) for vitamins A, D, and E, and for the minerals copper, iodine, selenium, and zinc. These vitamins and minerals, however, must be in a specific balance for the Silky Terrier to use them.

The nutrients found in the Silky Terrier's native environment of Australia would have included the meats from mutton, fish, and domesticated poultry. Grains and vegetable crops included wheat, rice, potatoes, and greens.

I recommend food sources of poultry, lamb, fish, wheat, and dairy products as the ideal base diet for the Silky Terrier. I feel the worst blend for this breed would contain soy, yellow corn, horse meat, beef, or their by-products.

SKYE TERRIER

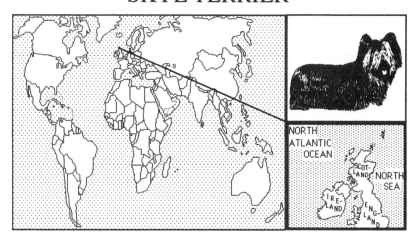

Weight Standards: m/f - average 28 lbs.
Height Standards: m - 10 inches, f - 9.5 inches
Coat: long and straight top coat, any color from cream to black
Common Ailments: kidney & liver failure, hot spots & skin rashes

The Skye Terrier developed on the island of Skye off the Northwestern Coast of Scotland. The records on this breed are complete and show that this breed has not changed at all in the last four centuries. It was kept isolated on the island of Skye and was not common to the whole of Scotland until the turn of this century. It then became a favorite of Queen Victoria and her patronage brought this breed popularity across Britain. Some unique physical characteristics of the Skye have also given it unique nutritional requirements. It is a very lean and muscular dog. It has a body weight to height ratio of about 3 lbs. per inch and its body length to height ratio is 2 to 1. This long and lean body not only gives it a unique appearance, but also a longer colon and a different muscle to body fat ratio than other breeds sharing same height or weight.

Native food supplies for this breed would have been land meats and ocean fish that were very high in fatty acid content. The meats would have been from the otter, badger, and weasel they hunted as well as ocean fish, poultry, pork, and mutton.

For the Skye Terrier I recommend foods that blend ocean white fish with horse meat, poultry, wheat, corn, and potatoes. They need to be very high in fatty acid content. I also recommend you avoid feeding this breed any beef, avocado, citrus product, soy, or beet pulp.

SLOUGHI

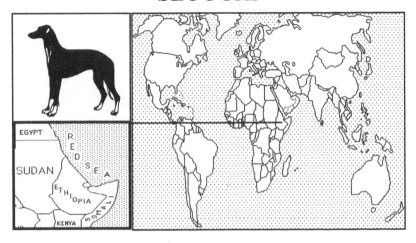

Weight Standards: m/f - 45 to 55 lbs.
Height Standards: m - 26 to 28 inches, f - 22 to 28 inches
Coat: single, smooth textured, in solid shades of sand or fawn
Common Ailments: bloat, PRA, circulatory problems

The Sloughi developed in the deserts of Ethiopia over 5000 years ago. They hunted Gazelles and desert rabbit for the nomadic tribesmen of the area. Then during the Middle Ages, when their Arab owners were invading Central Africa, this breed accompanied them to the area bordering the *Sahara* and *Tripolitania* . It is in this area where the largest numbers of this breed can be found today.

This breed has very little body fat. Its muscular frame is built for speed and it has a coat designed for living in a warm dry climate. I mention these physical characteristics because they are some reasons why the Sloughi must be fed a different type of food than a breed a heavy layer of body fat and a double thick insulating coat to protect its body from the cold.

Native food supplies for this breed would have been meat from the desert rabbit, gazelle, camel, goat, and sage hen. The vegetable crops would have been of a tuber type or low ground variety and the primary grains were rice and wheat.

For the Sloughi I recommend foods that are a blend of horse meat, poultry, brown rice, avocado, and wheat. However, I feel you should avoid feeding a Sloughi any soy, beet pulp, white rice, white potatoes, or beef.

SOFT-COATED WHEATEN TERRIER

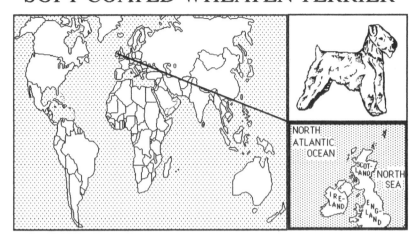

Weight Standards: m/f - average 35 lbs.
Height Standards: m/f - average 18 inches
Coat: long top coat, wavy & silky textured, solid wheaten in color
Common Ailments: liver failure, hot spots

The Soft-Coated Wheaten Terrier developed in Ireland prior to the 18th century. There is very little written about this breed prior to 200 years ago. Yet it is generally accepted that this breed existed in Ireland before the Kerry Blue (another Terrier of Irish origins). The Soft-Coated Wheaten Terrier's coat is its trademark and its namesake. The coat is both soft and wheaten in color. Even the pups born with a darker coat will change to this unique color of gold as they mature. This change in color can be used as a guideline for changing the food from a puppy formula to an adult maintenance formula. I mention this time of change since this breed is much slower to mature than many other breeds of the same body weight. To remove them from puppy formulas too early can harm them later.

Native food supplies for this breed would have been the same ones that come to mind when you think of Irish stew: a blend of lamb, carrots, barley, potato, and a slice of rye on the side. The other meats that they were exposed to were rodents and a very lean form of beef.

For the Soft-Coated Wheaten Terrier I recommend foods that use lamb, barley, rye, and potato. However, I feel you should avoid feeding any foods containing white rice, soy, or yellow corn to this breed. Also avoid any soy oil based coat conditioners. The oil based coat conditioners that are best for this breed have a base of linseed or wheat germ oils.

STAFFORDSHIRE BULL TERRIER

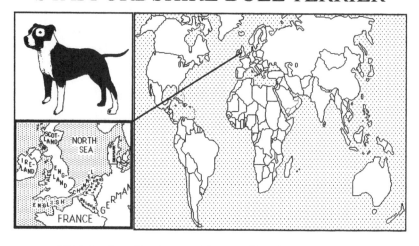

Weight Standards: m - 28 to 38 lbs., f - 24 to 34 lbs.
Height Standards: m/f - 14 to 16 inches
Coat: short and smooth, in all colors except black and tan or liver
Common Ailments: circulatory & respiratory problems, skin rashes

The Staffordshire Bull Terrier developed in England. It was named for the area were it was most popular. It is the oldest of all the Bull and Terrier breeds, including the American Staffordshire or Pit Bull and the English Bull Terrier. Yet ironically, this breed was the last of the Bull and Terrier breeds to be registered by either the Kennel Club of England or the American Kennel Club.

This dog developed from cross breeding dogs used in the blood sports of bull baiting and bear baiting. Today it retains the physical traits required to excel in the ring. However, the psychological mind set for being a champion in the blood sport ring was never a "trait of the breed" and each dog had to be trained in this skill. Without cruel blood sport training, this breed demonstrates a quiet trustworthy stable personality. Their gentleness with children, the elderly, and friends is legendary.

Native food supplies for this breed would have been those of the English country and consisted of beef, wheat, corn, potatoes, carrots, and cabbage.

For the Staffordshire Bull Terrier I recommend foods that are a blend of beef, wheat, corn, potatoes, carrots, and cabbage. However, I also feel you should avoid feeding this breed any rice (white or brown), soy, or avocado.

STANDARD SCHNAUZER

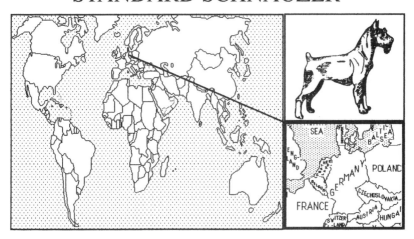

Weight Standards: m - 40 to 50 lbs., f - 30 to 40 lbs.
Height Standards: m - 18.5 to 19.5 inches, f - 17.5 to 18.5 inches
Coat: Hard & wiry topcoat, solid black or salt & pepper coloring
Common Ailments: dysplasia and tumors

The Standard Schnauzer developed prior to the 15th century in Germany. It is the oldest of all the Schnauzer dog family. Both the miniature and giant Schnauzer are its direct descendants. The breed was known in its native Germany as the "Wirehaired Pinscher Breed" until the late 1800's. They then became known as the Schnauzer when a dog of that name won top honors at an exhibition. This dog's name "Schnauzer" referred to a physical characteristic shared by all members of this breed; their whiskered snout. This breed has other physical characteristics that make it unique in the canine world. They possess characteristics like their sinewy and compact body or their seemingly unlimited reserves of energy. Like this breed's unique temperament and physical characteristics, they have specific nutritional needs.

Native food supplies for this breed would have been the same as those we associate with a heavy German meal today. The menu would consist of beef or pork, potatoes, carrots, and cabbage with rye bread on the side.

For the Standard Schnauzer I recommend foods that use beef, rye wheat, and potatoes. I also recommend that you avoid feeding any food containing soy products, white rice, or avocado to this breed.

SUSSEX SPANIEL

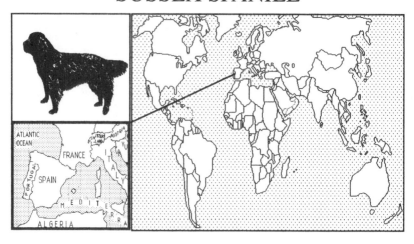

Weight Standards: m/f - 35 to 45 lbs.
Height Standards: m/f - average 15 inches
Coat: long and very thick, slightly wavy, golden - liver in color
Common Ailments: kidney and liver failure, hot spots

The Sussex Spaniel, as with most of the *Spaniels,* can trace its history back to Spain. Like most of the Spaniels that were taken from the continent to Britain, a lasting effect was made on this breed by the dog fanciers of their new homeland. An English dog fancier, Mr. Fuller, developed a line that had a very unique coat coloring. The coloring that Mr. Fuller's breeding program produced was a golden - liver. This is now considered to be one of the distinguishing features of a pure bred Sussex Spaniel today. This coat is also very thick in its texture as well as abundant in quantity. This coat gives the Sussex Spaniel a requirement for higher amounts of the amino acids Valine, Isoleucine, and Leucine than other breeds that have a thinner or single coat.

Native food supplies for this breed would have been poultry, such as woodcock and chukker (which have amino acid profiles high in Valine, Isoleucine and Leucine) blended with grains of corn, flax, and wheat. Vegetables included the potato, carrot, and beet.

For the Sussex Spaniel I recommend foods that contain poultry and a small amount of beef blended with potato, yellow corn, and wheat. However, I also feel you should avoid feeding a Sussex Spaniel any white rice, soy (which is very low in the amino acids Valine, Isoleucine and Leucine), or ocean fish.

SWEDISH VALHUND

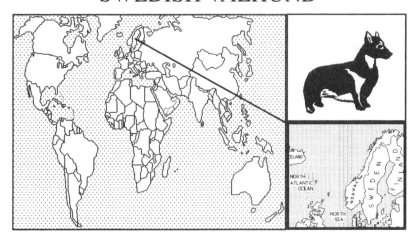

Weight Standards: m/f - 20 to 40 lbs.
Height Standards: m/f average 13 inches
Coat: double, thick, in gray or red sable coloring
Common Ailments: hot spots, skin rashes, kidney & liver problems

The Swedish Valhund (*Vastogotpet*) developed in the areas bordering the fiords in the cold and rugged land of Sweden. They are a member of the Spitz dog family. They were also the companions of the Viking tribes that inhabited this rugged country as far back as the 9th century. The Swedish Valhund (Vastogotpet) stands only 13 inches high but can weigh 40 pounds. When compared to the world wide "average 40 pound dog" that stands 19 inches in height, one can see many physical characteristics that give this breed different nutritional requirements than other breeds. Their long body gives them a longer colon than 40 pound breeds with shorter body lengths. Their heavy layer of body fat gives them different requirements than 40 pound breeds that are leaner. Their thick double coat requires different amounts of amino acids, vitamins, and minerals than 40 pound breeds with a thin single coat.

Native meat supplies for this breed would have been North Atlantic fish, reindeer, and bear (all high in body fats). Vegetables were of the tuber type with a grain that could grow in a short growing season.

For this breed I recommend foods high in fat and low in protein from food sources like fish and horse meat blended with wheat, beet pulp, and potato. However, I suggest you avoid feeding a food that contains soy, white rice, or citrus products of any kind to this breed.

TIBETAN MASTIFF

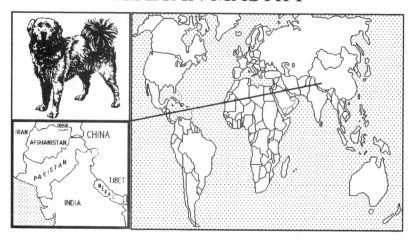

Weight Standards: m/f - over 175 lbs.
Height Standards: m/f - over 27.5 inches
Coat: thick, double, medium length, black or black with tan or gold
Common Ailments: dysplasia, hot spots, pigmentation problems

The Tibetan Mastiff developed in the foothills of Tibet, China. These foothills have an average elevation of 16,000 feet above sea level. This high elevation environment gave the breed its thick coat and a layer of body fat not found in the Mastiff breeds of the lower elevations and warmer climates. The high elevation environment also affected this Mastiff's nutritional requirements, making them as different from their English or Neapolitan relatives as their respective coats and coloring. The first written records pertaining to this breed appeared in Chinese literature around 1121 B.C. Later, when Marco Polo was in the far east he referred to this breed in his reports. These two early accounts provide evidence that today's Tibetan Mastiff has changed very little over the last 3000 years.

Native food supplies for this breed would have included meats of the horse, mountain goat, yak, llama, and oxen. The grains and vegetables are those that can grow in a very short season in rocky soil, like barley and rice or a tuber root that can be compared to our sweet potato. The Tibetan Mastiff has a dietary requirement for foods high in animal fat. They will not do well on the vegetable fats I recommend for its Neapolitan relatives.

For the Tibetan Mastiff I recommend foods that contain horse meat, barley, white rice, and beet pulp. I also recommend you avoid feeding this breed any potatoes, citrus products, avocado, or ocean fish.

TIBETAN SPANIEL

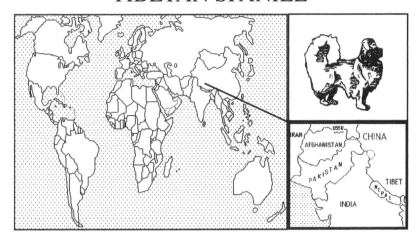

Weight Standards: m/f - 9 to 15 lbs.
Height Standards: m/f - average 10 inches
Coat: double, silky textured, top coat is long & lays flat, all colors
Common Ailments: kidney stones, liver failure

The Tibetan Spaniel developed in Tibet before the Shang Dynasty in 1100 B. C.. The records show that they have been bred pure in this part of the world since that time. In the canine kingdom this breed can claim to be one of the oldest pure bred dogs in the world. It is one of the few breeds with the *Spaniel* nomenclature lacking any lineage to Spanish origins. In the Middle Ages French literature described a dog called an *Epagneul* as comforter and companion to ladies of the Oriental courts. Somehow this *Epagneul* became the modern *Spaniel* part of this breed's name. An indoor dog, this is the only breed from Tibet that has a "hare foot" (the two center toes being long). All the other Tibetan breeds have the more compact "cat foot" shape, better suited for walking in the snow.

Native food supplies for this breed would have been from an environment with an average elevation of 16,000 feet above sea level. The domesticated meat animals are Yak, Llama, and Oxen. The grains and vegetables are those that can grow in a very short season in rocky soil, like barley or a tuber root that can be compared to our sweet potato.

For the Tibetan Spaniel I recommend foods that contain horse meat, barley, white rice, and beet pulp. I also recommend you avoid feeding a Tibetan Spaniel any carbohydrates from white potatoes, any citrus products, avocado, or any ocean fish.

TIBETAN TERRIER

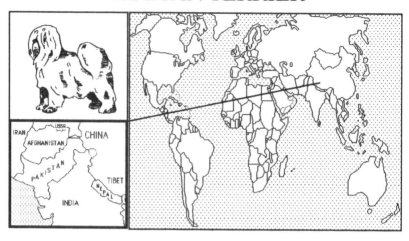

Weight Standards: m/f - 22 to 23 lbs.
Height Standards: m/f - 14 to 16 inches
Coat: double, long top coat; both top and undercoat are fine textured and profuse, all colors except chocolate are acceptable
Common Ailments: eye problems, hot spots

The Tibetan Terrier originated in the Lost Valley of Tibet. It was considered a good luck dog and was often given as a gift to a traveler who successfully made the hazardous journey into this remote Tibetan valley. They were never sold since this could tempt fate. Their homeland valley is high in the Himalayan Mountains and the floor of this valley has an elevation of 10,000 feet above sea level. This environment gave the Tibetan Terrier both unique nutritional requirements and some unique physical characteristics. A British dog fancier, Dr. Greig, brought some to Britain after he came across this unique breed of dog in India. In Britain they were called a Terrier because of their body size. However, it should be noted that the only similarity they have to any other breed that bears the name Terrier is their size.

Native food supplies for this breed would have been from an environment where the meat animals are Yak, Llama, and Oxen. The grains and vegetables are those that can grow in a very short season in rocky soil like barley or a tuber root that can be compared to our sweet potato.

For the Tibetan Terrier I recommend foods that have a base from horse meat, barley, white rice, and beet pulp. I also recommend you avoid feeding a Tibetan Terrier any potato, citrus product, avocado, or ocean fish.

VIZSLA

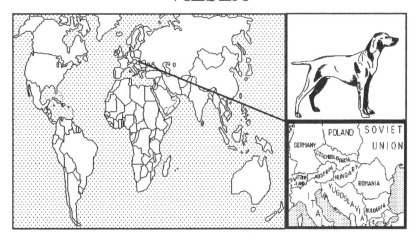

Weight Standards: m/f - average 50 lbs.
Height Standards: m - 22 to 24 inches, f - 21 to 23 inches
Coat: short but very dense, fine textured, in a golden rust color only
Common Ailments: dysplasia, skin rashes and hot spots

The Vizsla developed in the Great Plains area of Hungary on the border of Rumania. This breed of dog hunted both upland game and waterfowl since it was first bred pure in its native land. The breed suffered great losses between the two world wars of 1914 and 1939, and by the end of WW II in Hungary (1941) the breed was almost extinct. Saved by local dog fanciers, it is now back as one of the most popular breeds in Hungary and is honored as their national dog.

Native food supplies for this breed would have been from an area of continental Europe long known as the food basket of the continent. Over 90% of the land in the Great Plain of Hungary is under cultivation with 60% of that land being set aside for grain production. The crops of wheat, barley, rye, and oats are the principal grains produced. The most prevalent meats are from cattle, pigs, sheep, and poultry.

For the Vizsla I recommend food that is a blend of poultry, wheat, barley, and rye mixed with a second food that is a blend of horse meat and oats. This will give the Vizsla the high fiber and balance of protein it requires. However, you should avoid feeding them any food that contains soy bean products of any kind (including soy oil coat conditioners), white rice, avocado or beet pulp.

WEIMARANER

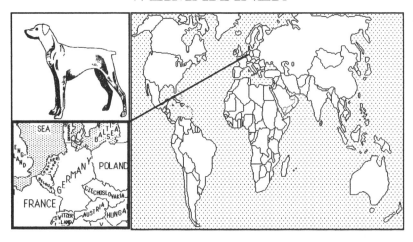

Weight Standards: m - 70 to 85 lbs., f - 55 to 70 lbs.
Height Standards: m - 25 to 27 inches, f - 23 to 25 inches
Coat: short sleek and gray in color
Common Ailments: bloat and dysplasia

The Weimaraner developed in Germany during the late 1700's and early 1800's in the Weimar Court, a township in the foothills of the German Alps close to Bavaria. Originally called the Weimar Pointer in their native land, they hunted the wolves, wildcats, mountain lions, and bear from the surrounding mountains. After these animals of prey became rare or extinct in the Weimaraner's native area, the breed then hunted the smaller fur bearing game and upland game birds of the area. They excelled as a bird dog because of their very soft mouth and were well established as a retriever for both upland birds and waterfowl when they first entered this country.

Native food supplies for this breed would have been from the Weimar Township area of Germany. The soil here is not noted for its fertility and has a unique mineral content. I associate this soil's unique mineral content with this breed's unique mineral requirements. Food crops of the area include the potato, cabbage, alfalfa, and barley with meats like pork, poultry, beef, goat, and deer.

For the Weimaraner I recommend foods that are high in animal fat from lamb and poultry. The overall food blend should be poultry first, lamb second, potato third and then a blend of grains like wheat and barley. I feel you should avoid feeding a Weimaraner any ocean fish, beet pulp, white rice, or soy.

WELSH SPRINGER SPANIEL

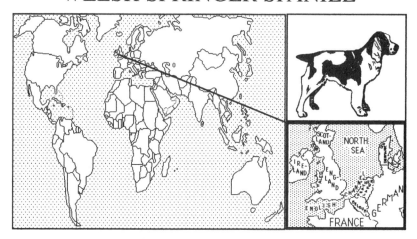

Weight Standards: m/f - average 40 lbs.
Height Standards: m/f - average 17 inches
Coat: flat, silky textured with mild feathering, red & white in color
Common Ailments: epilepsy, hot spots and skin rashes

The Welsh Springer Spaniel developed in Wales, which is located on a peninsula of Great Britain. This breed is a direct descendant of the red and white dogs that the *Gauls* brought to Wales in pre-Roman times. In Wales they were isolated from the rest of the world and bred pure for centuries. Wales has been described as a highland country of old hard rocks. Yet this country, which is only 150 miles long, has three very distinct climates. The Welsh Springer Spaniel comes from the higher elevations of Wales (2700 to 3500 ft.) in the Brecknock area. This specific area of Wales has a great deal of temperature flux. It was this environment that gave this breed a weather resistant coat that is "self cleaning". It was also this environment that gave this breed its unique nutritional requirements.

Only a limited variety of crops (rye, barley, wheat, and potato) could grow in the rocky soil of this breed's native environment. Any meats of the area were from the small herds of cattle or sheep and domesticated poultry, or wild fowl.

For the Welsh Springer Spaniel I recommend foods that blend poultry, mutton, and beef meats with corn, wheat, and potato. However, I also recommend that you avoid feeding any ocean fish, white rice, avocado, or soy bean product to this breed.

WELSH TERRIER

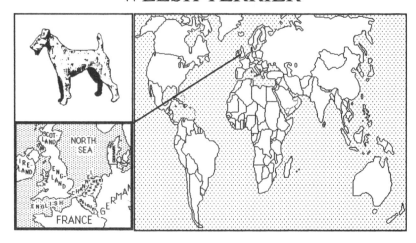

Weight Standards: m/f - average 20 lbs.
Height Standards: m/f - average 15 inches
Coat: short and wiry in texture, black & tan or grizzle & tan in color
Common Ailments: skin rashes, liver failure, kidney problems

The Welsh Terrier, a true *Terrier* in every sense, is a direct descendant of the old English Black and Tan Terrier. It was first discovered in the early 18th century in the country of Wales. This breed of Terrier developed along the Welsh coast to hunt the otter, fox, and badger that inhabited the rookeries of this north Atlantic land. They are very similar in appearance to the Airedale Terrier, from Yorkshire County England, except for their body size. This similarity has led to the speculation that this breed and the Airedale may be related. However, there are records dating from 1737 that show the Welsh Terrier to be bred out of the old English Black and Tan and bred pure since then. If there is a relationship between the Airedale Terrier and the Welsh Terrier, it is far enough removed so that we can identify each one for the individual that it is.

Native food supplies for this breed would have been from the coast of Wales and included the otter, badger, fox, fish, poultry, mutton, cabbage, and potato. These foods are the dietary staples for both the humans and the dogs in this area.

For the Welsh Terrier I recommend foods that are a blend of fish, mutton, poultry, corn wheat, and potatoes. I also recommend you avoid feeding any horse meat, avocado, citrus fruit, or white rice to this breed.

WEST HIGHLAND WHITE TERRIER

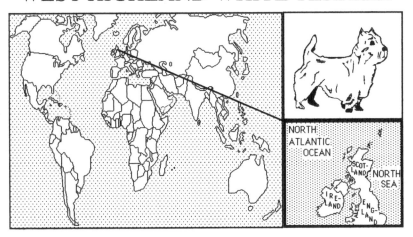

Weight Standards: m/f - 15 to 18 lbs.
Height Standards: m - 11 inches, f - 10 inches
Coat: double, hard textured, straight and always white in color
Common Ailments: coat pigmentation, kidney and liver failure

The West Highland White Terrier comes from the Western Highlands of Scotland and they are white in color. This area is described as hard rock formations bisected by valleys known as "glens" or "straths." The highlands are in the shadow of the Grampian Mountains. Though this land is not good for agricultural crops, it is inhabited by many crofts (small farms), which raise sheep able to survive by grazing amongst the rocks. Also living amongst the rocks are many vermin, such as the fox, rabbit, and rodents. These vermin can ruin the limited crops grown in this area. Therefore, the farmers from this area developed a breed of dog that would both help control the vermin population and save their crops. This special breed is today's Westie.

Native food supplies for this breed would have been the crofts' mutton and poultry stock, with potatoes and a limited amount of barley and rye. The dogs also would have eaten the vermin they hunted.

For the West Highland White Terrier I recommend foods that provide meat protein from poultry and lamb, the carbohydrates from potato, barley, and wheat, and the fats from their poultry meat source. I also recommend you avoid feeding a commercial food that contains soy, white rice, yellow corn, beef, or horse meat to this breed.

WHIPPET

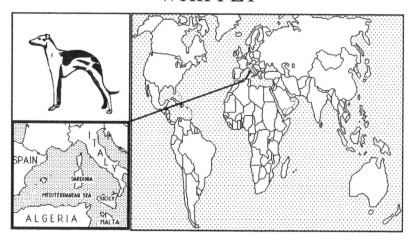

Weight Standards: m/f - average 25 lbs.
Height Standards: m - 19 to 22 inches, f - 18 to 21 inches
Coat: short and sleek, may be any color or color combination
Common Ailments: Monorchidism, hot spots and skin rash

The Whippet developed in Great Britain but originated in Italy or Northern Africa. Roman legions brought this breed to Great Britain when they invaded in 49 A.D.. The Whippet is the breed example I use when asked how long it would take a dog to change its nutritional requirements when exposed to different foods. My answer is that it would take as long as it would for a dog's coat to adapt to a new climate. After twenty-one centuries, the Whippet still has a coat best suited for the warm and dry environment of its origins and not the heavier double coat found on breeds originating in the colder climate of the British Islands. Likewise, they still retain the nutritional requirements they developed in their native environment. Fortunately for the Whippet the rabbit was the main food supply in both their native area of the world and in their new homeland.

Native food supplies for this breed would have been rabbits, domesticated poultry, mutton, goat, and wheat or corn.

For the Whippet I recommend foods that are a blend of lamb, poultry, wheat, and corn. The addition of a linseed oil coat conditioner to this blend will provide this breed with a good balance of the fatty acids its skin and coat require. However, you should avoid feeding a soy oil coat conditioner to this breed as well as any soy bean meal in its food. Other food sources to avoid feeding a Whippet include horse meat, beef, or ocean fish.

WIREHAIRED POINTING GRIFFON

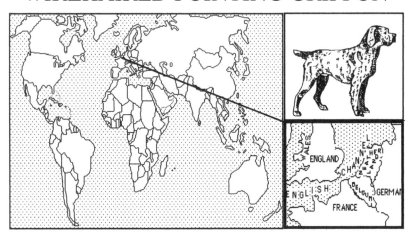

Weight Standards: m - average 60 lbs., f - average 50 lbs.
Height Standards: m - 21.5 to 23.5 inches, f - 19.5 to 21.5 inches
Coat: double, short, wiry textured, chestnut or gray & chestnut mix
Common Ailments: dysplasia, liver and kidney problems, hot spots

The Wirehaired Pointing Griffon originated in Holland and then developed further in France. Holland, now known as *The Kingdom of the Netherlands*, is a small European coastal country, north of France and east of Germany. Its highest elevation is 1000 feet and its lowest elevation is 20 feet below sea level. Holland's extremely fertile land and extremely wet climate produced a breed of dog that has one of the most unique coat fibers found in the canine family. This breed's coat, though relatively short, insulates the dog's body better than many fine textured long double coats found in the Nordic Spitz breeds. Yet this coat requires stripping and the texture is like that found in many terrier breeds from other climates. This coat, found only on the Wirehaired Pointing Griffon, is one way this breed is different from other breeds of canines. The differences among this breed and others also extend to its nutritional requirements.

Native food supplies found in their original coastal and lowland environment would have been oats, potato, rye, sugar beets, and wheat. Meats were from domesticated poultry, dairy cattle, and ocean fish of the North Sea.

For the Wirehaired Pointing Griffon I recommend foods that contain ocean fish, poultry, and dairy products blended with potato, oats, and sugar beet. I also recommend that you avoid feeding yellow corn, avocado, soy bean meal, or horse meat to this breed.

XOLOITZCUINTLI

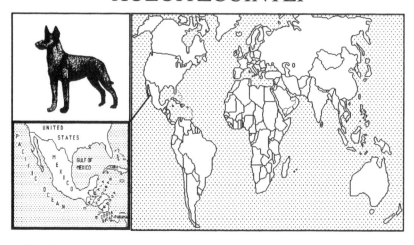

Weight Standards: m/f - Standard; average 50 lbs., Toy; average 30 lbs.
Height Standards: m/f - Standard; 13 to 22 inches, Toy; under 13 inches
Coat: a hairless breed of dog, only a tuft of hair on head and tip of tail
Common Ailments: depigmentation, albinism, cryptorchidism, and monorchidism

The Xoloitzcuintli (pronounced: show - low - eats - queen - tlee) developed in Western Mexico. Historians trace this breed of dog to the Colima culture between 900 and 300 A.D. The Colima people kept the Xoloitzcuintli as a representative of their god Xolotl. It had the duty of guiding the souls of the dead to their unearthly destinations. The Xolo has many unique features when compared to other breeds of the canine family. They are hairless and their skin will sunburn. They have an abnormally high body temperature due to a metabolic rate different from any other animal. Another interesting feature is the absence of the pre-molar teeth. All of these unique physical features make this animal a one of a kind breed of dog.

Native food supplies for this breed would have been from the western mountains of Mexico, located near the equator. This is a very hot and humid area where the native meats (even the wild boar) are very low in body fats and the crops consist of citrus fruits like the mango and papaya.

For the Xolo I cannot recommend any of the commercial food blends. I do recommend that you study the nutrients of their immediate area before you attempt to take one of these dogs home with you. The Mexican government has declared it illegal to take one out of Mexico. Try to meet dietary needs by providing native nutrients to any "exported" member of this breed.

YORKSHIRE TERRIER

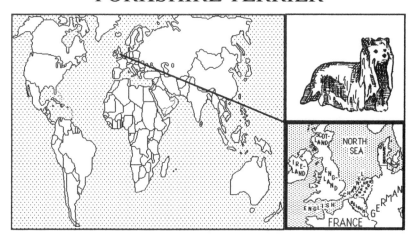

Weight Standards: m/f - under 7 lbs.
Height Standards: m/f - under 7.5 inches
Coat: double, silky long straight top coat, steel blue with tan
Common Ailments: slipped stifle, enclampsia
(common when whelping)

The Yorkshire Terrier developed near the township of Yorkshire, England, on the British Islands. Prior to their becoming house pets, they were used as ratters in the coal mines and mills of the area. During this time the average Yorkshire Terrier weighed around 15 pounds, (about twice the body weight of today's Yorkie). Today's small Yorkie became the most popular toy breed in England after they were selectively bred down in size and made into fashionable house pets. The Yorkshire Terrier is one of the "slowest" of the toy breeds when it comes to the development of its skeletal structure. Thus it requires more of the nutrients found in puppy formulas for a longer period of time than the other toy breeds. When first born, they are normally a solid black color and do not become steel blue and tan in color until they reach about one year of age. This change in coat color can be used as a "gauge" for changing the dog's puppy formula to adult dog food.

Native food supplies for this breed would have been rodents, a dairy cattle form of beef, potato, sugar beet, rye, and barley.

For the Yorkshire Terrier I recommend foods that are a blend of horse and beef meats, sugar beet, potato, wheat, and barley. I also suggest you avoid feeding a Yorkie any red fish, such as salmon, yellow corn, or soy.

Medical terms

Assimilation - *Process of transforming food into a state suitable for absorption by the circulation and conversion into body tissue; synthetic or constructive metabolism; anabolism.*

Bionutritive - *Affording nutrition. The sum of the processes concerned in the growth, maintenance, and repair of the living body as a whole. Biological nourishment provided by food.*

Black Tongue - *A disease due to a deficiency of niacin; similar to pellagra.*

Bloat - *An abnormal accumulation of gas in the stomach or intestines, resulting in distention of the adbomen.*

Cataracts - *Partial or complete opacity of the crystalline lens or its capsule.*

Collie eye - *Congenital defects of the choroid or optic nerve impairing vision.*

Cyst - *A comining form denoting likeness to or connection with a bladder or cysto. A membranous sac serving for the reception of fluids or gases.*

Dermoid Sinus - *A draining cyst originating at or near base of spine.*

Dysplasia - *A gradually crippling abnormality of the hip joint.*

Dwarfism - *Abnormal development of the body; the condition of being dwarfed.*

Eczema - *An acute or chronic, noncontagious, itching, inflammatory disease of the skin. The skin is reddened, the redness shading off into the surrounding unaffected parts.*

Enclampsia - *An after-whelping disturbance in a bitch's calcium metabolism characterized by nervousness and spasms.*

Heart Failure - *The syndrome resulting from failure of the heart as a pump. The mechanism is varied, the symptoms depending on whether the left or right ventricle preponderantly fails. Dyspnea is most marked in left ventricular failure; and engorgement of organs with venous blood, edema, and ascites, most marked in right ventricular failure.*

Hemophilia - *A sex-linked, hereditary disease occurring only in males but transmitted by females. It is characterized by impaired blood coagulation, attributed by some to a deficiency in the plasma of effective thromboplastinogen.*

Hot Spots - *Inflammation of the epidermis with loss of coat.*

Hyper Thyroid - *An abnormal condition brought about by excessive functional activity of the thyroid gland.*

Hypo Thyroidism - *A morbid condition due to deficiency of thyroid hormone; in advanced form expressed as cretinism or myxedema.*

In vivo - *In the living organism: used in contrast to* in vitro: *In glass; referring to a process or reaction carried out in a culture dish, test tube, etc.*

Kidney Failure - *The syndrome resulting from failure of the kidney as a productive gland.*

Liver Failure - *The syndrome resulting from failure of the liver as a productive gland.*

Monorchidism - *Congenital absence of one testis. Failure of one testicle to descend into the scrotum.*

Progressive Retinal Atrophy (PRA) - *deterioration of the retina of the eye.*

Slipped Stifle - *Dislocation of the kneecap.*

Snow Nose - *Inflammation of the epidermis in the nose region affecting the senses of touch, pain and temperature.*

Temperature Sensitive - *Variations of body temperature through the day.*

Torsion - *A twisting of the intestine following bloat.*

Tumors - *A swelling. Specifically, a new growth of cells or tissues characterized by autonomy, that is, independent of the laws of growth of the host. It is progressive and in malignant form limited only by the nutrition provided by the host.*

Von Willebrand's Disease - *An inherited blood disease somewhat like hemophilia.*

Worms - *A member of the phyla Annelida, Nemathelminthes, or Platyhelminthes. The medically important forms belong to the last two phyla.*

Each breed of dog has
physical or temperamental characteristics
that are different from any other breed.

The question is
NOT IF *those characteristics affect*
a breed's nutritional requirements,
BUT HOW MUCH *do they affect a*
breed's nutritional requirements?

William
D.
Cusick

& *two friends*

This is Mr. Cusick's second book. His first book about the different dog breeds and their very different nutritional requirements was, <u>CANINE NUTRITION & CHOOSING THE BEST FOOD FOR YOUR BREED OF DOG</u>, published in 1990.

Mr. Cusick first became interested in the nutritional variations between the different breeds of dogs in 1968. At that time he was the owner of a major West Coast vitamin manufacturing company producing an all breed dog food supplement that Saint Bernards thrived on but which caused nutritional distress when fed to Dalmatians.

His curiousness about the reactions that these two breeds of dogs had to the one food product led him on a twenty year search to identify the nutritional morphologies for most of the members of the species: canine.

After his research proved why a food "good for one breed can be harmful to a different breed" Mr. Cusick felt compelled to educate all dog owners about his discoveries. This book is only one way he is trying to get that message out. He has also taken his crusade on-line with an Internet web site titled "William D. Cusick / The Animal Advocate." His web site can be found through the various Internet search engines so that people can contact him with any questions they may have about breed specific nutrition and feeding their pets - CORRECTLY.

DORAL PUBLISHING

American Cocker Spaniel	$28.50
The Basenji - Out of Africa to You	$29.75
Beagle Basics	$21.95
Best Junior Handler	$16.95
The Border Terrier	$28.50
Born to Win	$39.95
Candle, a Story of Love & Faith	$ 5.95
Canine Nutrition	$21.95
Canine Source Book — 4th Editon	$26.50
Basenji, Stacked and Moving	$21.95
Ebony and White	$21.95
Enjoying Dog Agility	$26.50
Fido, Come!	$26.50
Great American Dog Show Game (Hardcover)	$26.50
Great American Dog Show Game (Softcover)	$12.95
How to Help Gun Dogs Train Themselves	$19.95
The Griffon, Gun Dog Supreme	$34.95
The Hijacking of the Humane Movement	$17.95
Healthy Dog	$ 6.95
Versatile Labrador Retriever (Hardcover)	$28.50
Versatile Labrador Retriever (Softcover	$23.50
Louisiana Catahoula Leopard Dog	$19.95
The Magnificent Collie (Hardcover)	$28.50
The Newfoundland (Hardcover)	$34.95
The Norwegian Elkhound	$28.50
Pooches and Small Fry	$15.95
Ready, Training of the Search & Rescue Dog	$26.50
Sieg the Magnificent	$13.75
Standard Book of Dog Breeding	$26.50
Winning With Pure Bred Dogs (Hardcover)	$26.50
Winning With Pure Bred Dogs (Softcover)	$23.50
Yes Virginia, There IS a Pet Heaven	$12.95

To Order, Call Toll Free: 1-800-633-5385

Visa - Mastercard - American Express Cards Accepted